CONQUER THE SYSTEM

MR VINCENT SCIALLI

ISBN: 1494951088

ISBN 13: 9781494951085

Library of Congress Control Number: 2014901079
CreateSpace Independent Publishing Platform
North Charleston, South Carolina

"This book is dedicated to all those people out there striving to succeed. A special thank you to my friends, colleagues, co-workers, employees and the many other people I have encountered in my life that have taught me and continue to teach me the lessons of success. To my wife Michelle, and my daughters Sofia and Isabella you are fuel to my success .... And finally thank you Dad for making me always want to be the best, and Mom for showing me how."

Vincent Scialli

FORWARD
FROM A FRIEND

Never having been asked to write a forward for a book before, the first thing I did was hit the Internet and Google up what goes in to a good forward. The answer was fairly straightforward. First tell people who you are, second tell people who the author is and what your relationship is to he or she, and third tell people about why the book is so great and why they should take the time to buy it and read it. So in that order, here goes...

I am a plastic surgeon. I have been for over 25 years. I am also currently the CEO of an international pharmaceutical company and have been the CEO of other companies in the past. I have several degrees, have traveled a lot of the world, been a pilot, a scuba instructor, and spent a lot of time with people that are at the top of the ivory towers in investment banking on Wall Street and Park Avenue, and have had the privilege to meet and become friends with some of the most successful people in the world. That said, who do I prefer to hang out with?

There is a saying that "water seeks its own level." I think that is absolutely true in friendship. You gravitate toward people you relate to. Some of the best times that I have had have been with Joey Concrete, Franky Trees and Vinny The Plumber (The author of this book). I met Joey when he was on his hands and knees building a brick hearth around my stove. Frankie does the landscaping around my house, and Vinny moved some pipes in my kitchen just last week. Yes, they are a brick mason, landscaper and plumber. So the next question one might ask is "what's the connection? Are you slumming?"

The problem here, is that some people are in desperate need of a trip to their eye doctor, because they can't see the level of the water that's in front of them. To invoke another old saying, "you cannot judge a book by its cover!" Even if these three guys were tradesmen and tradesmen only, that would not mean that they weren't interesting, intelligent, honorable, great friends and fun to be with. In this case however, the tradesmen story is a bit different. The only thing tradesmen about them is the clothes they wear. In reality they are just as business savvy and successful (if not more) than most doctors and lawyers that I know.

Joey Concrete started as a brick mason and now has many trucks and crews doing very large projects. Franky Trees took his father's landscaping business and built it into a mini empire. He now owns several buildings, plots of land, a tree service company, a mulch company, the nursery that supplies his new construction business and has essentially built a vertical monopoly in the industry. Vinny, took his father's one-man plumbing business and built it into one of the largest in our area. From being the area's authority on super high-tech, high-efficiency boilers to large construction plumbing, he has taken this business to meteoric levels.

Vinny's parents came to this country from Italy. From a long line of hard-working Neapolitans and they were so proud that Vinny was the first in his family to have a college degree. Armed with his newly-minted mechanical engineering degree, he went off to work for a large consulting firm in Manhattan. After a successful suit and tie career in Americas corporate world, one day,

Vinny called his father and said "Dad, you're going to kill me, but I want to go into to the plumbing business!"

At first glance, you could see why his parents would think he was crazy. Vinny understood though, that it wasn't the business you were in that made you hugely successful or not. Instead, it was the level to which you took it. In order to achieve his success, Vinny combined his mechanical engineering education, with street smarts, common sense, an incredibly strong worth ethic, and a huge amount of testosterone.

"Conquer the System" is an astonishingly well-organized analysis of what it takes for any individual working at becoming more successful at any level in their career. Vinny describes real world issues that we are all faced with and how to handle them with some straight up talk mixed in with his own life experiences. It contains great advice about how to think, plan, act and most importantly interrelate at multiple levels as you strive to succeed in business.

The writing is down to earth, and there were many times that I found myself thinking that while I never thought of it that way, Vinny's theories were both solid and sensible. The best part about it, was you felt like you were at a college lecture given by a combination of Archie Bunker and a character out of a best-selling mafia novel.

I highly recommend this read, as no matter what you strive for, either personally or in your career, this book is packed with solid advice that was both professorial and fun to read.

Joel R. Studin, MD, FACS

FORWARD FROM
A READER & BELIEVER

As a young, hungry individual with the desire to succeed I have seen real world results from "Conquer the System". I have applied the theories as both an employee and eventually an entrepreneur (look for the upcoming book "Creating the System")

I can say without hesitation that what is taught in this book is undeniably beneficial and will not be explained to you in any typical business school textbook or "path to success" book. What this book cannot do is create the ambition or desire for success in those who "don't have it in them" but for those that do (and clearly you do if you are reading this) it can spark that internal desire for success and give you a clear path to "Conquer the System"

If you have ever had the internal desire to succeed, regardless of the task you are attempting, you know that along with the insatiable desire for success you also need a game plan, or path for navigating the "system" as it is known. Any successful individual will tell you that you need a little bit of luck, lots of hard work and timely advice along the way. However by identifying the system that you are working within you give yourself a greater chance of achieving your individual success.

"Conquer the System" identifies the components and ideologies that structure corporate America and entrepreneurial small business and gives those within the system a foolproof method to navigate through the system and ultimately conquer it.

Whether you are a recent business school graduate just entering the corporate world or a seasoned employee tired of mediocrity, "Conquer the System" will show you the how and why behind what drives the system and how to approach each individual component.

The theories are explained using simple, real-world scenarios that everyone encounters at some point or another in their life. Common, yet often controversial topics such as how to ask for a raise and how to deal with backstabbing co-workers are addressed in these real world, situational examples that will have you recalling your own memories and feelings when you experienced that very situation, only now you will be armed with the tools to control the situation and ensure the outcome works in your favor.

As the chapters progress you will continue to relate to the individual scenarios and understand that the theories being described are not all that complicated, and while rarely revealed in a comprehensive manual, they are all supported by successful businesses all around us. The proof is undeniable and reaffirms what is being identified and described.

I wish you well in your journey to succeed and remember to not only read the book but believe in what it tells you. It worked for me.

Anthony Westenberger
NYU Schack Institute of Real Estate, Master of Science in Real Estate Development 2013
AMW Development, President

INTRODUCTION TO CONQUER THE SYSTEM

In every person's life, at one time or another, they feel that they have some sort of intrinsic information they must share with the rest of the world and feel compelled to write a book. I guess I have hit that patch in the road of life where I believe I can share some of my own life lessons, and hopefully, help someone just like myself somewhere else in the world.

I want to share my journey, one that began in my early years working in America's corporate world through to today as a small business owner. I want to detail how my experiences, coupled with my parent's work ethic, helped shape my view of business and how it should be conducted. By reading *Conquer the System*, you, like me—the so called "Average Joe"—can apply some of these techniques and improve your life by either advancing your career or advancing your own business.

One might ask: What in the world does a 40-year-old know about business and careers? Honestly, I don't know more than the next guy, but what I do know is that reading books on how to succeed written by those who are already successful in their own minds or in their wallets usually leads to a pretty boring book.

Like many naive people before me, I thought that going to work or starting a business was as easy as going to the nearest book store and buying a best-selling road map to personal success. Unfortunately, most of those books (many of which I have read), consist of self-absorbed multi-millionaires or wannabes who think the purpose of the book itself is their real reason for their wealth.

I strongly believe that people do not like tedious lectures, but find it easier to learn through stories based upon the experiences of others. I am writing this book from the perspective of a blue collar guy who was raised by immigrant blue collar parents who sent me into an unknown white collar world. It is written with simple words ... simple words that make up simple stories.

And just why should you listen to me? As long as I can remember, being the son of immigrant parents, I was taught *"If you wanted to be successful in America, you had to work!"*. No matter what happened the night before, the next morning you had to get up and go to work. It is called "work ethic." Many of us today simply lack this work ethic, may have lost it, or never had it to begin with. I have watched my father get up at 6:30 a.m. and work a 12-hour shift until 6:30 p.m. every night, from Monday to Saturday, for the past 40 years.

Building my own personal work ethic started with my earliest childhood memories of school. No matter what tricks I tried, my parents made me go to school. When at school, I needed not waste my time, my teacher's time, or my parent's money by not learning something. I needed to learn. The harder I worked at school, the more I learned, and the more I learned, the easier things became.

When I graduated college with a degree in Mechanical Engineering and landed my first real job in the corporate world, I applied the same work ethic that I was taught early on as child. While at work, the learning never stopped. Each job I held, I tried to squeeze every last ounce of information out of it for my own mental database. I asked questions, lots of them … sometimes too many of them in fact. I listened and watched closely on whom the key players were, just why they were the key players, and how they and the company were making money. The company I worked for had a set of rules and parameters in place to maximize profits and maximize the output of their workforce. I called those rules "The System."

My parents were immigrants. They were rural farmers from Italy, and in Italy, farmers had no System. Their System was survival. They worked the land to eat and understood the harder they worked the land, the more they ate. It was a "put in/get out" mentality built on the strength of their own backs. Don't get me wrong, my parents did not do so badly in this country with that mentality. They succeeded because they outworked those who were already here who lacked true work ethic. Even today, most labor-intensive occupations—many of which Americans find beneath them—are being done mostly by immigrants.

As my time in the corporate world progressed, the more I realized that true success for any one individual was based on either how they fit into their company's System, or that individual went out and created a System of their own. The better the System that was in place, the more efficiently things ran and the more profit was generated. When the System is implemented correctly, it brings immeasurable success to those who create it. All successful companies have a System in place, and this methodology allows their executives to constantly re-define and tweak the System. The firm's managers implement and enforce this System, and in turn, their employees can follow its path to success.

When I look at the work ethic my parents instilled in me and couple it with learning my company's System, I felt that I was unstoppable in the corporate world. Success at any company hinges upon what you learn and what makes up the System, and how to safely navigate it in order to maximize your own success.

This book's purpose is to provide that guidance you will need to navigate towards your own success. Our America has created an invisible System that we willingly and unwillingly follow and navigate, day in, day out. No matter where you turn or where you work in this country, there is a System in place to be followed. If you can correctly identify exactly what comprises your company's System and use some of the techniques I will outline in this book, I am 100 percent positive that success lies just around the corner.

Like I said before, I have read numerous books in life on people professing and proclaiming success and how to achieve success according to them. Most of them just put me to sleep with their boring dissertations and lectures. This book is intended to be an easy read with the use of everyday words and everyday stories, not corporate jargon that may lose your interest. Most people, including myself, find it easier to remember things when they are associated with something like a particular story, experience or situation. This is called "memory by association." Why do you think the Bible was written with so many stories and parables? It made it easier for the Average Joe to remember the true meaning of the Bible's teachings through these narratives. This too was my intention in this book. *Conquer the System* will give you some stories and situations that will assist you when encountering similar situations in your own life.

Each part of *Conquer the System* caters directly to where you are right now in your business life, and can act as your personal reference guide to achieving both your immediate goals and the long-term goals you may be striving for down the line. You can read any chapter of this book you would like first, or you can turn directly to a chapter for some quick advice for the specific situation you are in.

Let's be realistic here ... very few people in this country attain the unimaginable wealth like those we see in Fortune 500. The rest of the population, myself included, either has a job or runs a small business. In both cases, many of these Americans would really like to improve their lives slightly for the better. Most of them are not looking to be zillionaires, but are looking for a little help improving on what they already have.

What is interesting is that financial gain sometimes is not always the sole motivation for people to make changes in their lives. Today, more than ever, quality of life factors like improved self-respect, more time spent with the family and improved health have become just as important. When one improves their quality of life, it can bring happiness to a once unhappy person. When people are happy, they always prosper, no matter what they do, which often leads to financial gains.

By improving your business life, you can and will change your personal life as well. The two work directly proportional to one another, like Ying and Yang. However, each one will sometimes require sacrifices from the other in order to achieve a better balance of that Ying/Yang relationship. You may ask, "How can you achieve a better Ying and Yang? Isn't that a perfect balance?" Simply add a little bit of money to a balanced life and a better Ying/Yang is born. Maybe it's me, but people just smile more when there is a little extra money in their pockets at the end of the week.

Let us now embark on this mission of improving lives. With *Conquer the System*, read my stories and remember them, follow some of the advice set forth before you, and apply them into your everyday work life. If it works for you, then pass it on to a friend to better improve their life. The key is to better those around you as you better yourself. As your success grows, your views begin to change and the friends who refuse to change with you towards bettering your lives will no longer have a place for you on a daily basis. Success is contagious, and you will unintentionally surround yourself with people with the same drive and motivation as you have.

Good luck and enjoy. Make sure you send me along some feedback, including your own experiences and stories.

CONQUER
THE SYSTEM

The "System"

"No System, No Success!!"

Why do certain individuals or companies make lots of money while others make none? Why is it that no matter how hard my parents and others like them work, their rewards are far less than the effort they are putting in? What is the missing link to success that both effort and work ethic alone could not solve? Why do so many experienced individuals continuously fail to identify and implement the things that are making their competitors successful? Why do some make it look so easy, while so many other struggle?

As early as I can remember, I have been obsessed with finding the answers to these questions. Every day, I walk into businesses or meet business owners and analyze how they operate, make money, if they are profitable or not, and what they can do to make more

1

money. I ask many questions of these owners, both the successful ones and those who are struggling, and determine why each of their businesses are in the economic situations they are in.

For years, I believed that it was the product or the industry that guaranteed the success of the business, but over time, I realized I was dead wrong. Many business owners have good products with great ideas and are in great industries, but even with all those factors being equal, some just cannot achieve their full potential. Most are stuck in the hamster wheel by their own doing and only a select few have truly figured out how to harness the power of their business to achieve true wealth.

Here is a story about my Uncle Chris. He owns and operates a small sandwich shop in the neighborhood. He makes a great sandwich and runs a pretty good store, but never makes more than an honest paycheck. He has been in the deli business since the 1980s, and nearly three decades later, he's still slicing bologna. Ideally, his goal (and the goal of any owner) was for the business to eventually run itself. However, in his case and like so many others in the same boat, his days have grown longer and harder with each year that passes. He complains that the help is getting worse, the competition is fierce and operating costs are rising faster than what the market is willing to pay for a sandwich.

Consequently, in the same 30-year span that Uncle Chris sat making his own sandwiches, Subway has become the largest franchise (based on locations) in the world. Why is this so? Uncle Chris and Subway both make sandwiches, so what's the difference? Why is one owner worth billions of dollars with a private jet, while the other can barely afford to leave the store unsupervised for more than five minutes?

Is it because the quality of the sandwich is better at a Subway? No way! My uncle produces a much better sandwich by using the best ingredients. Is it because the managers and employees are better at Subway? No way! No need for managers. My uncle "the owner," by himself, works at the store all day, from opening to closing. He makes the sandwiches, he watches the register, cuts down on the waste, monitors the employees, and does anything and everything to make a profit at the end of the week. In his eyes, he runs his store at optimal performance in the way only a hands-on micro manager owner/operator, like him, could do. So with all of the positives that Uncle Chris has in contrast to Subway, why is it that they turn a much larger profit, while using inferior ingredients, with less experienced employees, and are run by absentee owners? Just what has Uncle Chris been missing after all these years?

Examples like my uncle are everywhere. America is filled with millions of overworked small business owners, those who are working for a paycheck rather than running a company. Take a look around ... how many people like my Uncle Chris do you know? It's not just about sandwiches either. Examples range from office supply firms, pizzerias, hamburger shops, clothing boutiques, hardware stores, software providers, construction suppliers, taco stands, and any product or service you can think of in this world. The products are like any other basic commodity ... like selling "bottled tap water" or a simple service like picking up dog poop. There are millions of industries in society today, but only a select few are making lots of money, while many more are failing miserably.

The question I keep asking myself over and over again is: "Why does it have to be so hard for Uncle Chris and others like him while it seems so easy for a select few? Think about it ... Fred DeLuca, the co-founder and president of Subway, wasn't a rocket scientist. He didn't invent anything, cure anything, create the sandwich or even perfect the sandwich. Sandwiches were around thousands of years before Subway, yet he is still a billionaire today. How did the man take a $1,000 loan from a family friend and a couple of slices of bread and parlay it into largest franchise in the world? The answer to that question is the Holy Grail for guaranteeing success for all businesses and their employees.

After nearly 30 years of my own research in both working for business owners, then in my own business, and now listening to business owners, I believe I have found the answer to that question: "The System."

So, what is this System?

"It is a set of standards (procedures, rules, guidelines, laws, criteria, etc.) that simplify the complex nature of any business to maximize the output of its workforce for the sole purpose of providing exemplary service to its customers, while guaranteeing a profit.

The System achieves the goal by creating a simulated reality for its employees and customers where both parties know what to expect from one another during their experience together. It is this pleasurable experience that reduces customer anxiety, guarantees repeat business and perpetuates a cycle of success.

The system can be written and/or unwritten. It can be rigid and/or fluid. It can be tangible and/or intangible. The system is the backbone to any successful company. No matter what the business is, if it's successful, then it has a 'System' in place."

Have you seen the movie The Matrix? There is a scene in the movie where you see a green binary code on the screen, which is supposed to represent a computer program that runs in the background creating the surreal world that the characters live in. The way I see The System is similar to what The Matrix represented in the movie. Let me explain.

Do you remember the premise of the movie? If you are one of the few who has not seen the movie, the premise is as follows. There are a group of intelligent machines that create a software program called "The Matrix." This Matrix program creates a fictitious environment, aka "simulated reality," for unknowing humans to live and prosper in. In this simulated world, the humans go about their everyday lives as if it was real, but in reality, they are not in that world but rather fed that image via The Matrix program.

The reality is that humans are not in a world as they know it, but are living in pods whose sole purpose is to create electrical energy from their bodies so that it can be harvested and used to power to the same machines creating the program. The result is a perpetual cycle of unlimited energy for the machines. If you haven't seen it, then you need to rent the movie to see how it all ends. In the meantime, let me incorporate this premise into the business world by using Subway again as the example.

Subway, the corporation, is the intelligent machine, and the System they have in place creates the simulated reality for customers like you and me who eat there. If you don't think it's a simulated reality, then answer this one question: Why do all of us, especially in unfamiliar areas, drive past local eateries like my Uncle Chris's deli to get to a place like Subway? The answer is that they have made us believe that they are the only ones who will give us a good sandwich, at a good price, with good service, in a clean store. Our expectations tell us exactly how the sandwich should taste, where the order counter is, what items are on the menu, what the store should look like, where the bathrooms are located and what to hear from its employees, before we even walk in the door. Is that reality? If you say "Yes," then you are saying that all other sandwich shops cannot give you what Subway can. You know that is not true at all. In fact, there are many small shops in the same vicinity as Subway that can exceed your expectations, but the anxiety of the unknown keeps you from entering those doors.

Subway's System, just like The Matrix, makes it seem to its customers that their goal in the sandwich world is to provide the perfect lunch experience. In fact, their true goal, like any company, is turning a profit for the Subway Machine. Their simulated reality takes total control of its customers experience once they walk through that door. The result is a satisfied customer based on their own preconceived experience crafted by the same company making the sandwich and the profit.

I knowingly fall victim to this simulated reality every day. I will drive on an empty tank of gas and pass a generic gas station just to get to a national chain like a Hess or an Exxon. Even though gas is gas and I run the risk of running out of gas before reaching my destination, I still take the risk. Why? Because I know what to expect when I get there.

Another funny example of this is when I take a long road trip with the family. My wife and I noticed that we always stop during the drive to eat at McDonald's, even though I never eat it when at home. Why? Because there is no reason to stop and take a risk on an unknown roadside restaurant in an unfamiliar place when I know exactly what the French Fries taste like at McDonald's.

Walt Disney was the king of simulated reality. Have you ever been to a Disney theme park with its own surreal town? I remember last year taking the ferry from the parking lot to the Magic Kingdom. A tourist next to me explained that Walt wanted the parking lot far away from the Magic Kingdom, and he purposely made it accessible by either ferry or monorail only. He wanted his guests to use the time on the ferry as a cleansing process of forgetting their reality in that parking lot and replacing it with the joys of his world that lie ahead. Not sure how true the story is, but I will tell you I found myself smiling like a six-year-old when I saw Cinderella's castle from afar. He opened the doors to his land of make believe and we, in turn, open our wallets and made him a very rich man in return.

Companies invest billions of dollars annually to constantly perfect their Systems. The better they create this simulated reality for its consumers, the more money they make. It is this money that perpetuates the cycle of their own success. If they continue to keep their customer's anxiety down, they will not go elsewhere, and their company continues to get stronger.

All successful Systems are made up of two major parts, an exoskeleton and the endoskeleton. The exoskeleton of a System is what all customers experience from the outside looking in. It's the facade to the structure of your business. This is what customers see and come to expect from you on a daily basis. Successful Systems like those of Subway, have exoskeletons that are strong, stable and are close to impenetrable. They re-invest millions upon millions in marketing to strengthen their exoskeleton, where no one incident or one customer could literally shut them down completely.

However, there is one factor that can take down even the most powerful of businesses with the strongest possible exoskeleton. That is a System with no endoskeleton in place. The endoskeleton of a System is the internal framework of any business that is required to be in place in order for the business to maintain an impenetrable facade and be successful. In other words, Subway is not successful by way of its sandwiches, nice stores and commercials alone. There is no way Fred DeLuca became a billionaire without creating a framework first. I personally believe that the endoskeleton must always be in place before attempting to solidify the exoskeleton. Just like when putting up a new home, the framework is what holds it up, even though neighbors only see the facade of the finished product.

What makes up the endoskeleton of any successful business system? These are the policies and procedures that all employees of that business must follow. This endoskeleton should be large enough to encompass each and every component of the business, no matter what it is. This means it can be a simple procedure as to how a floor gets mopped, or as complex as a corporate handbook or companywide training manual. The System must have something in place for almost any situation that may arise internally for that company. This will allow the decision-making to be made by the System and not be based on the judgment of one individual owner or manager.

Creating this type of structure also allows the owner to defer responsibility to its employees and yet still maintain control at the same time. With thousands of locations, can it be possible for Fred DeLuca to inspect every single one of the sandwiches that goes out the door? Absolutely not! However, the Subway System can with ease. Their System has a procedure, from the ingredients, to the baking of the bread, to the amount of cold cuts on the sandwich and how long it should take to make. It is this structure that can take a high school kid and plug him in as a sandwich maker with very limited training.

The endoskeleton is far-reaching in every aspect of business internal operations, and it is what people refer to all the time as the "Corporate Structure." That structure controls every aspect of an employee, from positions, pay scale, job titles, job responsibilities, raises, bonus, performance and anything else that allows a business to run on its own accord. The larger the corporate structure, the stronger the System gets and the bigger the profits grow.

A large endoskeleton should not be confused with a bureaucracy like big government. The size of the endoskeleton is confined to the size of the business it serves, and it should grow proportionally with the company. It is the duty of the owner to no longer micromanage, but rather, manage the System itself by creating, tweaking and modifying it accordingly. A System needs to remain fluid enough, and its owners, managers and employees still need to be held accountable for their actions when implementing it.

Bureaucracies and large endoskeletons that have outgrown their exoskeleton usually fail miserably. They are slow-moving in their decision process which makes them ineffective in the fast-changing, modernized world we live in. They become like stubborn old men locked in their ways, as they fail to realize that if they don't modify their System accordingly, their competitors will swallow them whole.

Good Systems reward great employees with promotions, pay increases and bonuses. They are incentive-based, not experienced-based. Employees move up not because they have been there long enough without being fired, but rather, because they are better at that position than the next guy. Meritocracy replaces mediocrity, and the System allows anyone willing to work hard free access to its corporate ladder of success.

By having a System in place that shares both an exoskeleton and endoskeleton, the end result is a business that can handle any situation that may arise. A business no longer has to rely on the decision of one owner, but rather, the System in place does it all by itself. The System does not sleep, does not take a day off, does not come in late, and is always there … 24 hours a day, seven days a week, just waiting and willing to make you a success.

My Uncle Chris never spent the time in developing a System for his deli. He spent all of his time making sandwiches, but never a day or minute creating a System required for him to grow. He figured, if he did it all, then the sandwiches would always be right and the customer would always come back. However, he never realized that he would always be limited to what he and his eight hours could do in a day and that was it.

When he trusted an employee enough, he taught that person everything from top to bottom, like a miniature version of himself, and in the process, made his employee a future competitor without ever realizing it. The better he made that one person, the more money that one person wanted, and because he didn't have a System in place to promote expansion, his one business alone could not sustain the pay of two owners. The result was that employee leaving and opening up a few miles away in direct competition with the guy who taught him everything.

In the beginning of his career, if my Uncle had slightly eased up on his hands-on approach and invested a few hours a day writing down and implementing what he knew all along, he would have unknowingly developed a System of his own. No matter how small of a business he was in, if he had at least one employee, then he would have been creating policies and procedures for that employee.

Over a small period of time, the System would have grown with the employees, and each and every one of them would have been exposed to the same exact training as the next. He too would have found it easier to train employees to follow one procedure within the System, rather than learn everything about the business. The end result would be a workforce based on the System and not on whom the owner deemed responsible.

In short, corporate America is filled with hundreds of thousands of successful companies—both large and small—employing millions of people every day. Each of these companies, regardless of the consumer base they serve, all have a System to call their own. It is up to each of you within these Systems to learn how to navigate and be successful within them. In this book, I have provided you with the information needed to succeed in any corporate System, regardless of where you are within it at the moment. If you read it thoroughly, get motivated and put in the work, then your ascent up the corporate ladder is destined to happen.

In my next book aptly named *Creating the System*, I will provide those of you who have decided to venture into a business of your own all of the components you need to develop a successful System. In *Creating the System*, I will delve deeper into the two endoskeleton and exoskeleton parts of a successful System, and which companies have perfected them and how to create them for own business.

The goal in both books will be to provide you with all of the tools necessary to succeed at any level in any business, no matter if you are the owner or the employee ... to take you out of the hamster wheel that you are in currently and put you in the sports car of your dreams. Remember, the ride is just as amazing as the destination. Success awaits you and good luck.

CHAPTER 2

Your (My) "First" Day

"Each day is a day closer to the inevitable."

If you are nervous on your first day of a new job, you need to realize that everyone at your company is also feeling the same way you are. Your first day of work is also your company's first day of accepting you into their presence. It is very crucial in those first few days that you make the right impact on those who directly correlate to your success at the job. Accepting their System and the players who control their System will guarantee you success at your company.

I remember my first day of work like it was yesterday in the big city of New York, one block over from Times Square across from Bryant Park. I was 23-years young, full of energy and decked out in a three-piece suit, with an empty brief case, train pass and scared shit.

My journey to America's corporate world began much earlier than that first day. It began the day I was born to two immigrant parents who just came to this country from their homeland of Italy. I was the firstborn of my parent's entire family lineage in the United States. It meant from that day forward, I would be the first child to speak English, the first to go to school, the first to go to college and eventually, the first to enter into the corporate world. Throughout the years, there were many firsts for me, and being nervous was and always is a part of my life.

My entire family came from a small southern town in Italy where the goats outnumbered the inhabitants. The tiny town of Durazzano sits quietly nestled in between olive grove-laden mountains and a valley with fields of vineyards. There were no traffic lights, no cops, no supermarkets, very few cars and a few phones. They lived off the land they owned. They were raised on the "put in/get out" work mentality, which meant the more they "put in" physically, the more they would "get out" of the land they were cultivating. The crops they cultivated were immediately eaten, jarred and stored for later use, or used to feed the animals. The animals were grown, eaten, and their byproducts were used for clothing, soap and many other household items. Nothing was wasted, and nothing was taken for granted. It was and is the simplest System that we know in the world today. This System is what we call "Survival." They had true hunger, and in Durazzano, it was work to live as the alternative was to starve to death. They had no other options at the time; even education (which was private and expensive) had to take a back seat to working the land. The physical work was obvious, but the mental strength they developed in those fields was the most valuable tool they passed on from generation to generation.

In their society, the alternative was starving, so they only knew one way ... the way of work. There was no TV, no Internet, no movies, no cell phones, and none of the distractions we have today. Having no distractions meant more time to "FOCUS." Focusing on the goal of farming and harvesting, coupled with a dedication to "WORK," guaranteed a healthy family.

Their days consisted of waking up at the break of dawn, tending to the animals, and heading to the fields to cultivate their land. They put in hard hours until dusk and headed home where they prepared food and reaped their rewards. Everything, and I mean everything, at their dinner table came directly from their own hard work, from the wine, the oil, the breads, the cheeses ... even the clothes on their backs were hand-sewn, and the wood for heating and cooking had been cut with their own hands. The next morning, they would repeat the process, and over and over, from generation to generation, their simple System became the foundation to all successful Systems of the world today. Life in my parent's world 60 years ago was simple, and however simple it was, there is no denying the two basic principles of their success: Work and Focus.

In the 1970s when my dad was in his early 20s, he, like many other Italians from his hometown, looked to the United States as the land of opportunity. He was part of the second migration of Italians to hit this country almost 100 years after the first migration which occurred before and during the Industrial Revolution. This second migration in the 1970s was different from the first. The United States was a world super power, an industrialized nation that was ready to accept those willing to put in hard work. There were Systems in place already so that any immigrant from any nation could come to the U.S. and be immediately productive in American society. That was the American way, and it was packaged with a nice little slogan called "The American Dream."

In America, everything you needed to eat or wear was found on a rack or on a shelf. There were no planting or harvesting seasons to worry about, no land to cultivate, no animals to slaughter, and no clothes to make. All fruits and vegetables from all over the world were always in season in America. Breads, cheeses and wines, etc. in all different tastes were always available at any time in America. Meats were packaged, eggs were in a box, and everything was disposable like utensils, cups, napkins and paper towels. There was gas for cooking, running water, hot water for showers, indoor bathrooms and electricity in every room.

America took everything my parents had learned to focus on and worked for and gave them easy access to it, either at a store or at home. America's genius was that it took my parent's thoughts of daily survival and replaced it with their personal wants. They no longer had to worry about growing food to eat, but rather, where and what store to go buy it from. It was a simple deductive process that led each immigrant, after a few months of living here, to realize that everything they ever wanted was available in this country. The more they liked the things that America had to offer, the harder they needed to work at getting them. "In America, you need to work!" was something my parents always told me. It was that simple.

Many Americans who were born here lacked the "wants" of my parents because of constant exposure to what America had to offer made them complacent. With so much at their fingertips, they became desensitized, causing them to lose "focus" and greatly reducing their will to "work." It led them to believe, as Americans, what they were given by this beautiful country was their right, rather than a privilege. The factory jobs (and many other labor-intensive occupations) that once proud Americans held strong in the 1940s and 1950s were now beneath this new work force. Regardless of the pay scale, Americans made it clear that immigrants were better suited to become the backbone of their own economy. Millions upon millions of immigrants from all over the world, including my parents, were all too eager to fill those shoes.

My parents, along with the immigrant population armed with focus, wants, and the will to work found it easy to prosper in this country. They found it easy to go to work and do anything in America when they no longer had to worry about their immediate survival. Sweeping floors or shoveling shit was easy compared to what they had endured in their country; there was no job that was beneath them. In their previous System of survival, they had been accustomed to just live, there was no hope for something greater. Instead, America provided them with security at home and in the work place, and our nation allowed these immigrants to hope for something greater. That hope let them forget about just living, and gave them the opportunity to focus on the things that they never dreamed about before, "A better life for them, and especially, a better life for their children."

As my mom fixed the knot on my tie and straightened out the lapel on my new pressed black suit, I could not help to think of the sacrifices they made to get me to this day. As I approached the front door, she handed me a gift; a leather Coach Attaché Case. After thanking her for the gift, I leaned over her tiny five-foot-nothing frame and kissed her goodbye. Like a typical Italian momma, her eyes swelled up with tears and she began to cry. In my heart, I knew her tears represented the years of hard work, dedication and sacrifice she and my father had made to get me to that point, and now, it was my turn to make them proud.

As I sat down on the 6:32 a.m. express train, I began to reflect of the impact of my first day had on the entire family. I thought about my dad who worked tirelessly and reflected on the story of him as 13-year-old boy being put on a train and sent into the city of Naples to work. The city of Naples back then was like sending a kid into the worst parts of New York City back in the 1970s, and it was no place for a little boy. There, he lived in a convent with his aunt, Sister Fiorenza, while working full-time as plumber, making lead pipes by hand. His childhood life was not easy, unlike what he made for me. To this day, he never really speaks about the things he experienced as a child growing up.

I couldn't help but get emotional thinking about at age 24, my father packed up everything and came to this country to start a whole new life. He left everything behind, so I (at the same age) would be able to and sit on the train with a new job, nice suit, and a college education.

My college education represented another major sacrifice in my parent's life for none other than the benefit of my own. In my first years of college around 1992, the economy had tanked and my father was faced with very little work and mounting bills, including my college tuition. Instead of having me get loans, he sold an investment property that housed his business office at the time, to cover the costs of my tuition. That piece of property was probably the only investment he ever made that made him a good dollar in rent, and because of me and investing in my future, he gave it away. I never forgot what he did for me. It became my motivation to show him a return on his investment by prospering at my new job. I knew that if I did well, then his investment in my career was well worth it, and I wasn't going to let him down.

I thought about my mom who came to America as a young girl. She learned to read and write English on her own by reading romance novels. Even though she and my father had grown up in the same town living about a mile apart, they never met until they both had immigrated to Westbury, N.Y. Mom was eight years younger, and her personality was the total opposite of my dad's. He was cool as ice, and she was the fire that kept him going. It wasn't until I lost my mom to cancer a few years ago did I realize her true impact on our family.

Typically in all Italian families, the family structure is called "Patriarchal," meaning the man is the head of the household. However, anyone who is a true Italian knows, that from the outside looking in, it's Patriarchal, but on the inside its 100 percent Matriarchal. Dad was the figurehead, while mom was the boss.

My mom was the backbone that my father lacked. She had no fear. She exuded confidence and demanded respect. Nothing was unattainable for her. She would always tell me, "You can do anything you want in this world, as long as you set your mind to it." She was the one who convinced my dad that he could get a plumbing license on his own even though he couldn't read or write English. She was the one who helped build his sewer business into a large company by 1981. Dad just wanted to work; he hated the "business" part of running a business. Mom handled the economics at home and at the office too.

When the sewer work began to dry up around 1984, my dad and his partner (who was also his best friend) parted ways. My dad was the licensed plumber, but it was his best friend who ended up taking the business in a sealed bid. The breakup wasn't an amicable one. On the very last day of operation as the last employee said goodbye, only my dad, his partner and his partner's brother in-law remained in the office. The brother-in-law, a huge guy over 300 pounds and over six-feet tall, locked the office door, and proceeded to physically assault my dad standing at five-foot, four-inches and 165 pounds. This guy, with the help of my dad's newly ex-partner and definitely ex-best friend, pummeled him with everything they had. I don't know how he got out of there, but all I remember was coming home from school, getting off the bus and seeing my bloodied up old man holding a .357 Magnum at the front steps ready to go back to the office to kill somebody. It took all the strength my mom had to convince him not to go back and he listened to her. She saved him that day.

After selling his company, I remember my dad not working and sitting on the couch for months on end, just sleeping his days away and constantly moping. He was severely depressed about being betrayed by his best friend and walking away from the company that he started. I watched my mom single-handedly build up this man who had been totally destroyed. Every day, she told him she believed in him, that he could do it on his own again, and he didn't need anybody else. Through her guidance, life came back to him, and in just a matter of a year, he bought his first plumbing van and Scialli Plumbing was back in business.

Dad was fragile. Mom was a beast. Nobody took advantage of her and the people she loved. If you were on her team, she was fiercely loyal and would sacrifice anything for your success. Her quick wit and sharp tongue made it difficult for any person to get an upper hand in any argument. As long as there was respect, then respect was given, and when it wasn't, then prepare for a battle. She never backed down when she knew she was in the "right," and it didn't matter who was on the other side of the argument. I am her.

Mom was and is everything to me, like every mom should be to every son. However, to me, she was more than just someone who gave me motherly love. She was my mentor in life. Dad worked, but didn't speak much at home. He was quiet, didn't mentor much, but expected perfection, a sometimes unachievable perfection at best. As a kid, I was hooked at being the best that he wanted, but it was my mom who actually taught me how to be my best. He wanted it, but she taught it. That was a big difference.

She showed me that no matter how unattainable my dad's expectations of being the best were, you still needed to go at each and every goal as if you were going to be the best. Not just go through the motions, but to go at it like a fierce lioness on the hunt to feed her cubs. The ferocity and intensity behind achieving every goal, through hard work, dedication and pinpoint focus on the task at hand … that was what she taught me. It didn't matter the end result, what mattered was giving it your best shot.

The greatest gift any parent can give to their child is not monetary or materialistic. Instead, it is to give them the "focus" and "work ethic" that they can use and implement for the rest of their lives. My parents blessed me with both of these traits, and through their sacrifices, I realized that not maximizing my own potential at this new job would not only be a lost opportunity for me, but a huge disservice to them. I was not going to let that happen.

Back again to my first day …

The train arrived at Penn Station and the mad dash of corporate life called the "rat race" begins with hundreds of thousands of suits moving in all directions, all with a purpose and a destination. There I was, standing at the platform with all the emotions running through my mind of what in the world am I going to do, so how am I going to act and what am I going to say in the corporate world? I had no formal training, no relative in the industry, no experience to draw from.

Walking out of Penn Station and into the streets of Manhattan, I stared straight up at the buildings around me for the entire one mile walk to my new office. The "City," as us Long Islanders call it, was huge to me. I felt that I was a tiny boat lost in a great ocean, with no idea what would happen next. The horns, the lights, the cabbies, the smells, everything was moving so fast around me that I believed I would never grasp the enormity of the "City," thus leaving me dazed and confused on every morning commute.

Once in the office, we were given the typical corporate orientation, which consisted of a history about the company, some human resources paperwork to fill out, and being introduced to some employees for mentoring. Corporate orientation is where they introduce you to their system, its components and its procedures. It is your sole task during the orientation process to correctly identify where your place is in their corporate system. Think of it as the System being the island, the buried treasure being the big salary, this book being the map, and your first day as the starting point. Once you know where you are with the company, then you can begin the process of ascension within its ranks.

The first few days are the easy part, this is where they want you to let your guard down and relax and get you slowly into the swing of things in your new job. The people around are all nice to you, and everyone wants to know about you and where you came from and so forth. The small talk you obligingly fall into will be first, and most importantly, last "impression" you leave with your colleagues for the rest of your corporate time there. That is why it is so crucial to bury the nervousness inside and exude confidence in your words and with your manners. Don't get arrogance confused with confidence, no one wants to hear how great you are, but you need to show them you are here to play and play hard.

You show confidence in many ways to your colleagues or superiors. One way is to speak clearly and always look at the person you are speaking to in their eyes. Always speak to people head on, eye to eye, and when shaking hands, do the same. Never look down or away when speaking to someone, especially when answering a question. Not looking at someone when answering, though you might be right in your answer, may by default, give the impression you don't know what you are talking about. When asked if you can add something beneficial to a conversation, speak up and let yourself be heard. At meetings, volunteer to present an issue, stand tall and speak to the group slowly, looking in different people's eyes to see if they are really getting what you are saying.

When you are walking in the office, always keep your head up and make as much eye contact with people no matter who they are and what their position is within the company. You should learn their names quickly, and always greet them with a hello and address them by their first name. From the security guard to the company president, you never know who you are going to need in the company at any given time to help you keep an edge or maintain an advantage on the rest of your colleagues. So always remember people's names, keep your conversations short and walk though the office like you always got something to do.

I learned quickly at my company that the people who presented themselves with confidence, no matter what their title was, got more respect in the office, got more done, and in turn, it reflected in their paychecks. It is very pivotal to your success to be confident at all times, and it is also important to understand that you cannot succeed strictly on confidence alone. Confidence is just one piece of the puzzle. There are more pieces that will be discussed in the chapters ahead.

On the train ride home, with my first day in the books, I could not help but smile. I had done it. For one day, I, the first Scialli, had joined America's corporate world. The weight of everything that had been running through my mind early that morning was released, bringing a subtle calm and peace to my being. I put my head back and joined the suits of world and slept all the way back home.

Your first day will be just one of many other first days in your life. Therefore, it is nothing to be nervous about, but rather, something new to embrace. Look back at the sacrifices and the sacrifices of your family, as I did, and use it as your motivation to succeed. Take what they taught you, "FOCUS" on your goals, and "WORK" with an unbridled passion in order to achieve them.

Now…Get focused and be ready to work hard and the rest will fall into place.

CHAPTER 3

Who Are You? The Horse Or The Boss?

"Take your blinders off!"

I t's amazing how many people wake up in the morning, perform the same mundane morning routine and go to work either unhappy or indifferent. Many of you know exactly what I mean because many of you feel like you're the person I just described. When you ask them about their job, they have no clue as to how they ended up doing what they are doing. Many of them don't know where they are going with their job either. There are also plenty of people in positions who were put there based on how they were perceived to be by their superiors. If you lack an identity in the System, then the System will make one up for you. Typically, this type of categorization ends up being the wrong fit for you, thus leaving you unhappy in that environment.

That is why it is so important that you categorize yourself in two major work personalities. Are you "The Horse" or "The Boss?"

The Horse is the personality type that likes to be given a task, and be left alone to accomplish that task to the best of their ability. This personality doesn't like adversity, and doesn't think outside the box. They have blinders on, and completing their task is all they want to do. They come in on time, do their job and leave on time. They are generally not too interested in overtime unless told to stick around, and are not interested in advancement other than their yearly review. They are mostly good people who treat the job as a job and nothing more. They like things simple and base their livelihood on what they make at their job. They enjoy the stability that the system brings and abhor adversity. This description probably makes up most of the corporate workforce in America. The Horse may be you. If it is you, then make sure the job that you are looking for you fits your goals from a standpoint of aptitude and attitude. In other words, can I do that job and will I be happy doing it?

If you think that you are The Horse, then be happy with minimal corporate movements within the system, and minor pay raises. Be happy with the fact that you will do the brunt of the work for your company, while others may take credit or make more money. The key to this is: *"If you are going to be The Horse, then be The Horse that wins the race."* There is nothing wrong with just wanting to do your job. There is nothing wrong in just finding a certain level of comfort and running with it. There are many people today who have been with the same company for 30 years, and some are doing exactly what they liked to do since the day they started. They are very successful in their own right. They have put their kids through college, paid off their home and retired with a nice nest egg. In their years at their company, they have probably seen the System spit out many Bosses, but they kept chugging along, like the work horse with blinders on. Horses usually move laterally in the system rather than vertically like their Boss counterparts.

In order for The Horse to be successful within the System, you need to follow these three basic rules.

The Three Rules of The Horse
1. Do your job and do it well.
2. Follow the instructions given to you.
3. Show loyalty to your company.

That means producing, not complaining, not whining and respecting your superiors. That will guarantee you job security for years to come. Trust me … do not look at this as a short-term thing. This is usually a life-long commitment. If you treat it as a short-term gig, and think of it in terms of, "Hey, it's a job for now," the System will snuff you out as soon as your company gets a little slow and they will hand you your walking papers in no time at all. Always follow the three rules stated above and don't rely on seniority because a smart company always has a younger work horse in the wings ready to replace a slower, more complacent and higher paid "Horse" like you.

If you don't fit in The Horse category, you must be a "Boss." It is so much more glamorous to be a "Boss" right? Well let me describe a Boss for you and see if it is really who you are.

First, the term "Boss" does not mean "the supreme being in the System." A Boss can be anywhere in any position at any time in any company. It's not just a title, but a way of being. How many times have you seen company Bosses by title only with little or no respect from their employees? Or, in other aspects, how many times have you seen a person with no title get more production than other guys with titles within the same System. All you need is two people doing something together and one of them, by default, is the Boss. The System requires Bosses. Without them, the System cannot evolve with time, cannot be implemented and cannot be enforced. Bosses exist at all levels within the System, and it's the System itself that will determine their success.

It is very important to understand that everyone wants to be "The Boss," but not everyone is truly capable of being one. The System, if designed correctly, will have its own checks and balances in place to determine if you are an effective Boss. It is corporate suicide to attempt the role of a Boss and falling flat on your face. In failure, you will lose the respect of your immediate peers, piss off your superiors and get crushed by the real sharks in your company who are more than ready and willing to replace you.

Being the Boss embodies a few characteristics that many have already been accustomed to. Most people know Bosses are more outspoken, more confident in their decisions, and quick to answer when rebutted. But, being a "Boss" at heart is deeper than that … it's a personality and a way of life. If you are a Boss at heart, then you already know it is easier to have a "Horse" to do the work for you. Your real calling is to be the jockey who rides the Horse in the right direction, at the right speed and brandish your whip at the proper pace in order to maximize output without killing the Horse. That's what a "Boss" is.

Another analogy can be made using a captain of a ship. Practically every aspect of the captain's ship is being run by the crew. The captain's sole purpose is to make minor adjustments to steer the ship and crew in the right direction. But like the captain on the ship, if you put yourself in the "Boss" position, then you must be willing to suffer the consequences if things go wrong ... just like when a captain goes down with his sinking ship.

Being the "Boss" requires you to go out on a limb, but taking that bigger risk by default will result in bigger financial rewards than The Horse. For example, when you are at work and your Boss gives you a task, look at the task as if you were in his position and how you could perform that task better, more quickly, and more importantly, more profitably for the company. Trying to be a Boss will always require you to work twice as hard as your colleagues. Bosses do not settle for mediocrity, they have pride and confidence in knowledge of the task at hand. Real Bosses make sure that they are at the top of their game at all times, meaning they put in the extra time when the Horses are home sleeping. Bosses are always thinking, always refining themselves, and are always looking for the next obstacle to tackle. And when they are totally satisfied with their current accomplishments, they start to look up the corporate ladder and slowly climb to get at their own Bosses. If their Bosses are not being the leaders we are describing, and are sitting back on their laurels, then they will soon be out of a job and replaced by the very employee they hired.

Its survival of the fittest in the corporate world, and those who make money for their company are considered the fittest. The System loves a dog eat dog mentality, as it keeps itself sharp and at the top of its game at all times by having the fittest employees as the Bosses. Real Bosses are not the proverbial fat man sitting behind a desk. Instead, they are everywhere around you and encompass blue collar workers as well. If you believe that you are a Boss, then you can act at any time as an extension of your own Boss. You can handle any situation thrown at you or at least hold on for the ride long enough until they get back. Boss-like personalities always make more money and move up the corporate ladder at a much faster rate than their Horse counterparts.

Boss personalities, should avoid three major pitfalls in order to be successful in the System. The first pitfall to avoid is "**Laziness.**" They should never give the impression of working less than their Horse counterparts. The term "work" does not always specifically mean the actual work being done. The System sees a Boss as a hard worker by specifically managing their Horses effectively and efficiently through planning ahead, assigning the correct Horses for specific tasks and making small adjustments along the course of the job to end up with a completed task in which both the Boss and Horse are comfortable.

The second pitfall to avoid is "**Complacency.**" I believe this is the greatest downfall of most Bosses. Do not grow complacent in your position, it will corrupt your aggressive style and you will eventually forget the hard work and dedication that got you to where you are in the first place, resulting in a lack of production of your unit, and inevitably, you being replaced. The Boss should never be thought of as being complacent because this will corrupt employees' work horse mentality and lead to an ineffective unit. Bosses should never forget that Horses have pride as well, and when they lose faith in their leader, they will stop producing, period.

The third and final pitfall to avoid is "**Getting Caught With Your Pants Down.**" What does that mean exactly? It means you need to be on your game at all times, no matter what position you hold within the company. If you are going to be the Boss in a situation, then know the task at hand well. You must be very good or very knowledgeable in the task at hand, and should have a certain logical process in your decision-making.

If a situation arises in which you did not make the best decision, a superior may ask you the simple question, "Why did you do that?" You need to explain the logical process as to how you came to your decision. Your Boss-like decision might not have been the right one, but if your explanation as to how you arrived at that decision makes sense, then they most likely will correct your logic and score big points with the Boss in the "Future Promotion" category. For an up-and-coming Boss, even making a bad decision warrants some credit because you are thinking outside the proverbial box. The worst thing to do is not to have a logical answer for your Boss as to why you did something. No matter how confident you may feel, if you cannot back it up, you are caught with your pants down and lose all credibility as a viable candidate for future promotion. If you try to cover your ass and attempt to lie your way out of a poor decision made, then you most definitely will be out of a job. Being a Boss requires leadership, even when the chips are down and how you respond to adversity will reflect on your success.

In conclusion, you must know by now if you are a "Horse" or a "Boss" personality. By reading this book, I am almost 90 percent sure you're a Boss or a future Boss, sharpening your business acumen. Just remember … there is a time and place for everything, especially in the corporate world. Nobody knows everything all of the time, and nobody makes the right decisions all of the time. Therefore, you need not be The Boss or The Horse in every situation.

You can interchange the two based on the task at hand, but when chosen, do it to the best of your ability and do not flip-flop between the two within the same task. You will undermine, confuse or distract the other Bosses and Horses around you. You cannot change your personality at heart, but you are not bound by it either. Be flexible and use each to achieve your long-term goals.

CHAPTER 4

Create Goals

"A lack of goals breeds complacency."

I f you want to succeed in the System you are currently in, then you need to create goals for yourself. If you lack goals, then there is no motivation to succeed within the System. The System loves goals, creates goals, and are the markers that determine who rises and falls within it.

A few years ago, I ran into an old childhood friend of mine named Peggy. We spoke for a while, and during our conversations, we reminisced about the old times. In conversation, Peggy had mentioned to me that she had found an old newspaper article of an interview that we did as classmates in third grade about what we wanted to be when we grew up. I asked her, "What did I say I wanted to be?" She was amazed that most kids in the class picked the usual profession of fireman, baseball player or doctor, but I clearly stated in that article that I wanted to be an engineer. It kind of shocked me also, because I didn't remember the article and how in the world did I know at eight-years-old that I was going to be a mechanical engineer many years later?

What I did know at a young age was that I liked to design stuff on paper and then build what I designed. My first-ever design was a street hockey net, designed and specified piece by piece on a sheet of loose leaf paper. And shortly thereafter, me and a bunch of friends gathered and cut the wood to the designed specs, and a few days later, we were playing street hockey. A few years went by and we realized that wood was too heavy to lug around and the nails wouldn't hold up to the constant moving of the net from home to the playground on a daily basis. So, it was back to the drawing board I went, and being that my dad was a plumber and the alternate material of choice was PVC pipe, a new pipe net design was created. My family, to this day, still speak of my design drawings of almost 30 years ago, and also convinced them then of my future successes.

What's the moral of the story? It is pretty basic. Create goals for yourself ... period! Know what you want and go with it. Many people don't know what they want, they are in la-la land going from job to job, career to career, or following the money train to the next big payoff that eventually never comes. In my little story, it showed how at an early age, I knew that I liked to design, create and build tangible things. I knew that engineers, in all aspects, did exactly that, so by default, I wanted to become one. I found my passion at a young age and then found the career that complemented that passion. As a kid, I didn't know or care about money, salary or being a boss ... I just wanted to be an engineer. As I got older, my primary goal of being an engineer may not have changed, but I starting adding short-term goals, long-term goals, refined and/modified existing goals, and even created daily goals.

What exactly is a goal? To me, it's a personal or professional accomplishment that can be achieved at any time based on the criteria set forth by the individual creating them. They are milestones or markers on your journey through life that your ego uses and compiles to create your self-worth, and in turn, creates a successful mindset.

No two people share all the same goals, quantity of goals and range of goals. Each person is different and their goals and mental makeup of these goals are just like their own DNA. It is my opinion that goal-oriented people are generally more successful in business and command higher salaries. If you ask your colleague about their goals in life and at work, you can get a pretty clear picture of where they are going in the company and if their System will have a place for them in the future.

Think of your goals as wipers on a windshield in a car, and life is the road you are driving on. Time is the speed which you are driving, while rain, snow, bugs and the wind are the obstacles of life ahead of you. The wipers give you clarity and the ability to see your destination. Think of your goals as the clarity to your own life. If you get an obstacle thrown your way, then there should be a goal in place to rid yourself of that obstacle.

Here is another quick story about my goals and an experience expressing them at work. In my first week at the engineering firm, I was invited by the CEO and other head honchos to a "Breakfast With the Boss" at the Princeton Club in midtown Manhattan. It was all of the EITs (Engineers in Training) and the CEO. We all took a seat at a roundtable with our nifty pressed suits anxiously awaiting the CEO's speech. Before he began his long-winded speech about how great his company was, I made sure I sat at the last seat closest to him at the table (never shy away and always stay closest to the boss so he begins to remember your face).

He began his story and explained the history of his colossal engineering firm which was started by his great grandfather, and then slowly got to asking all of us what our goals were at his company? He glances over to the first EIT at his left to speak and quickly went around the table, leaving me as the last one on the right to state their goal in the company. As they went around the table, I painstakingly watched each kiss ass give the same typical bullshit answer that the CEO wanted to hear. Each one would say, "My goal is to be a successful engineer in your company." I was thinking to myself, "What a line of shit!" When he got to me, I had to decide: Should I do the same or give him the truth of my real goal. In an instant, I thought to myself what the hell, let him hear it, he might always remember me for it or he can get pissed and fire me on the spot.

My answer to him was as follows, "My goal, with all do respect, is to own your company. That means working hard and not stopping until I have my name alongside your name on the office door." I could feel the tension of all the other EITs next to me thinking, "What the hell did he just say?" Instead, I smiled and went on with eating my breakfast as to say, "Hey, it's only normal to think like that." The CEO simply replied, "Vincent, if you work hard enough, I am sure that we can make some room for you." He didn't get upset. However, I do believe he was more shocked of my ambition than impressed by it. Little did he know if I had gotten to his level, I would have rubbed him out faster than a snitch in mobster movie. I always wanted my name on the door and mine only. Not his.

So now that you understand how goals are a vital part of your business success, let's get started on helping you create your own. If you already know what your goals are, that's great, but go through the exercise anyway. Maybe we can add a few more goals to your list or better categorize them for you. Here is the first step to creating goals. Take a pen and a pad and write down these two words "Career" and "Personal" at the top of the page and divide the page into two major columns.

Then, along the left side of those columns, break it into the next five major categories: Dream Big, Realistic, 10 Years From Now, Five Years From Now and Immediate. Remember these categories can be any choice of yours, but these are mine that you can start off with.

The table should look like what you see below:

Goal Types	Career(or Business)	Personal
Dream Big		
Realistic		
10 Years From Now		
Five Years From Now		
Immediate		

Once you have created a table like this, the rest is pretty self-explanatory. In "Dream Big," write down some of your goals in your career and in your personal life. It is good to dream big, its good for self-esteem, and it always gives you something to look forward to and strive for. I always say to my friends: "Shoot for stars, and if you land on the moon, it's not so bad after all. If you shoot for the moon right away, there is no place to go if you don't make it and you fall right back to Earth."

Here is another example. When we were young, my friends always said they dreamed of buying a nice car like a Mercedes. Instead, I would tell them I dreamed of owning the company itself. So fast-forward 20 years to today. Many of them have made it to the point where they could buy a Mercedes, in which they are content with that achievement. So their drive is gone. Some of my friends never achieved buying the Mercedes and have given up on trying. I, on the other hand, am still working on trying to buy the company, so my drive continues.

A few months ago, I went to visit one of my mentors in business, Andy Ceriello. Andy is also an Italian immigrant like my parents who owns a popular gourmet butcher shop in East Williston, N.Y. specializing in Italian foods. I worked for Andy part-time during my college years, making fresh mozzarella and Italian sausage. In those four years, he taught me more about business than any book, college professor or TV personality could ever teach me. His teachings are reiterated throughout this book, and I will forever be grateful to Andy.

During my visit, Andy told me that he was proud of the man I had become. He continued to tell me that he knew I would always be successful in his eyes. I asked him, "Andy, how did you know that?"

He replied, "You remember the little red Toyota you bought when you were working for me while you were going to college."

"Yes," I replied.

Andy responded, "Well, I asked you why in the world did you buy such a cheap car when there were so many nicer cars out there? And you responded … 'because if I cannot afford the car I really want, then I am not going to satisfy myself with a so-called nicer car, so the Toyota would do just fine.'"

He said he realized that complacency was unacceptable to me and I would always strive for what's better. That is why it is important to write down your wildest dreams of success.

In the second row, you have "Realistic" goals both for career and personal. This is where you can modify your big dreams to something more attainable based on your own realistic belief of your capabilities. Make sure that these goals are similar to your big dreams. If they are not similar, then you create a disconnect between the two, thus defeating the purpose of creating goals.

Remember, goals are like all the rungs on a ladder and the big dreams are at the top of that ladder. Therefore, you need each smaller goal to reach the main goal. For example, if your dream goal is becoming CEO of the company you work for, but realistically you look at yourself and where you are right now and write down a realistic goal: "Become the regional manager for my company," that's a more attainable goal in your lifetime. This step is still on the path of achieving your ultimate dream of becoming CEO.

Now, continue down and see where it says "10 Years From Now" and write your goal for what you want to achieve 10 years from today. Here, you may want to include goals like "Become the branch manager for my office." You cannot pick a goal like "Run a hot dog stand in 10 years" when your dream is to be the CEO of the local bank your working for as a teller right now. What does owning a hot dog stand have to do with becoming the CEO? Nothing! The two just don't mesh! This means the dream of becoming the bank CEO was never your real dream in the first place. If you really wanted to run a hot dog stand, then your real dream would be to "Live in Key West drinking Mohitos on the beach selling hot dogs to the tourists." The lack of connection between your goal 10 years from now and your dream goal will mean you will not achieve either one. You need to be true to yourself in what you want out of this little thing called LIFE. If your dreams are real, then working for them will never seem like work. They will become natural to your being.

Repeat the process of filling in the next row "Five Years From Now." Using the example of a CEO wanna-be, they would write: "In five years, my goal is to get a master's degree in business from the local college." That's the perfect goal for them, because they know that in order to achieve their other larger goals ahead, a college degree is a major part of the process.

Finally, your "Immediate" goals are by far the most important goals to your success. They are the ones that come first on the totem pole and have the most immediate impact on your self-esteem. It is very important to create and achieve these goals on a daily basis. Do you know why the faces on totem pole at the bottom are always grimacing? It is to symbolize that they are holding the weight of everybody else above. That's why the immediate goals are so important.

Back to the example of the CEO wanna-be ... their immediate goal can be making friends with their immediate boss, working late hours, coming in early, etc. These are the building blocks to achieving their dream, and by accomplishing these tasks on a constant basis, it increases their self-esteem and they no longer are goals. They become absorbed into their being, thus making room for more immediate goals.

The key to remember in creating goals is that it is never too late to start, and it is never too late to change your goals. Be true to your being and it will come easy, lie to yourself and you will never achieve anything. You might make money, or you may not, but you will never achieve "A better Ying and Yang: The balance of being happy in both your personal life and your career with lots of money!"

So go ahead and create your goals today! Writing them down is just to get you going, but I believe your goals are a part of you, and in no time, will not require any writing whatsoever.

CHAPTER 5

Know How Your Company Makes Money

"Is the CEO of Dominos the best pizza-maker in the business?"

Here is the key to making lots of money within the System and guaranteed career longevity: Learn how the System makes money, and become a part of that process. In turn, you will become a vital cog in the money machine in which your immediate bosses have no other choice but to promote you and compensate you as well. This is the most basic fundamental thing to know when working for someone. You will be amazed at how many people don't know this or care to know it.

Let's start with a basic example to better illustrate this principle ...

Say there is an owner of a small pizza shop in town with a few employees and three primary employees. What is the key to making money in this particular business? You might say, making a good slice of pizza at an affordable price and getting it out to your customers as fast as possible, creating turnover and maximizing sales and profits. In other words, sell more pizza and make more money. That's a pretty good business motto, but it is even simpler than that: It is service and making your customers happy. The pizza is the product, but you might as well be selling shoes, it really doesn't matter. It is a scientific fact that customers find their food to taste better when their service is better.

Now back to our example. There are three major employees: Tony "The Pizza Guy" who makes a good pizza and works night and day; Mario "The Host" who meets, greets and takes reservations; and Joe "The Counterman" who rings the register, orders the food and pays all the bills. At first glance, you figure that Tony "The Pizza Guy" has the most vital role, thus he must be the highest paid because you cannot have a pizzeria without a pizza man. Or, you might say Joe "The Counterman," the man who handles all the money in the business, has the most vital role because how can you be profitable without accounting all the numbers. If you picked both of these guys, you are wrong. When you peel back the layers and examine the core of a pizza business, the answer is that Mario "The Host" is the most important employee to the boss in the entire company. Why? Because he is a salesman. He meets his customers at the door, he welcomes them, speaks to them nicely and puts them at ease. He is there to accommodate the customers if the pizza tastes bad and if the bill is too high. He makes the company money. Like the composer of an orchestra, he makes music to the customer's ears, resulting in profits for the boss.

The other positions that Tony and Joe hold are infrastructure positions. Sure, they are important, but they are repetitive jobs that can be easily taught to someone else in due time. These types of employees can be easily replaced. Think about it ... a pizza guy just makes good pizza, but in theory, it's a recipe and a procedure that can be replicated. The counter guy who accounts for the company, he is strictly numbers, another mundane task which, in theory, a boss can find someone to replace. Don't get me wrong, this doesn't mean that the pizzeria can succeed without them. Absolutely not. The owner needs these good men or work "Horses," but the guy the boss absolutely cannot let go is Mario "The Host." Mario is the guy who all the customers come to see to eat a good slice and have a good time. Mario's sweet and fast-talking approach diffuses every bad meal into a happy customer, and correlates to big tips to the wait staff and big profits for the owner. He is the highest-paid employee in the pizzeria, and gets a bonus at the end of each year. The thought of losing Mario to a competitive pizza shop down the block has the owner talking partnership in a few years. You think I'm crazy right? Wrong. This scenario is seen in all businesses.

Staying with the pizza motif, I ask you this: Is the CEO of Dominos the best pizza-maker in the business? Nope.

Look at the company you work for. Are the smartest guys always the ones with the highest salaries in your company? Not likely. I remember in my engineering firm after a short time being there, I realized that some of the best engineers were in the same position 30 years prior, now working for the same guys they once helped train. The guys making the money quickly realized that the engineering company made money providing a specific service to its clients. They learned the System to find, make and maintain satisfied clients for their company who paid top dollar for our engineering services. Some of them had their basic engineering accreditations, but most of their offices were decorated with pictures and sports memorabilia they gathered from client trips, dinners and golf outings. Business deals were made on a handshake at the golf course, not because we were the best engineering company in the world. The best engineer was the man with the best Rolodex with the clients who had the deepest pockets. These guys were the rainmakers for their company, make it rain money with a few nights on the town with a couple of clients.

My own father is a perfect example of a person who never really grasped how his own company really made money. He is the best plumber and one of the smartest men I have ever known, but he is also the worst businessman I had ever known. Like I have written earlier in this book, my dad had been raised with a strong and solid work ethic, and was taught the "put in/get out System." My father's System was sweat equity, six days a week throughout his entire life. He never developed his System to go further than his own hard work. Like most old-timers, his System never accepted change, never allowed himself to change with the times, and never trusted any employee enough to do it for him. His belief was that he made money because he did impeccable work and that his work was guaranteed to last for years. His System was simple and sounded great and he made a decent living for a while. However, as time progressed, he found himself working longer and harder, and the money wasn't the same.

So when I took over, I realized he had built a great reputation, but there were many flaws in the System he created. Yes, he did good work, and good work is a premium that he never capitalized on. In a nutshell, he had poor purchase management, poor billing habits, poor organizational habits, poor scheduling, poor upselling skills, and in turn, it negatively impacted his cash flow as he was constantly working behind the eight ball. He was always chasing his earned money, and sometimes, had to let it go uncollected because he hadn't asked for it in such a long time.

You see, my dad always thought his customers wanted him and he personalized his business around that desire from his customers. In reality, that was his downfall as a businessman. Because he personalized his business with his customers, his customers automatically felt they deserved a discount or deserved to take their time paying him or not pay him at all. He was their so-called "friend," their "family plumber," and "the nice guy" you could call at any time and he would show up with a smile to fix your problem. The closer he was to these people, the less compelled he felt to charge them the right price and ask for his money when he did. He felt embarrassed to ask for what was rightfully his and thought that his good guy persona would be negatively affected if he pushed too hard. What he never realized and knew all along was that these people weren't his friends at all. If they had been his friends, they would have truly appreciated his work and paid him even before he asked for it.

What I told my dad the very first day of working with him was this. "Each person is a customer first and then everything else later ... customers pay the bills. Period." I continued by giving him the following example ...

Let's say your customer called about not having heat in one of his rental apartments, and you are on vacation or don't pick up your phone to respond. They will call someone else in a minute to get it fixed. When that "stranger plumber" shows up with his truck and gives them a price, they pay with no issues at all. Why? Because they don't know him, but they need him, and the "no heat" issue still needs to be addressed. You see, dad giving a good job is a bonus to them, but no matter what, they still need to get their problem fixed. My father, being a good guy, friend, cousin or whatever is irrelevant to the whole situation. They are customers first and if the industry's going rate is $125 per hour for service, then that's what they need to pay.

Good work, even great work, is what the customer expects all the time, and it is why they called my dad in the first place. But they must reaffirm his good work by paying him when he is done. What is their alternative for not calling my dad? They run the risk of bringing in a stranger and paying the same rate to someone who doesn't know the existing conditions, spending more time diagnosing the problem, and in turn, not ever fixing the issue correctly. After being burned a few times, you see how quickly that customer will come calling again.

It took a few years to modify his System, but each and every one of my dad's existing customers were retrained to look for Scialli Plumbing when they had a problem and not look for Neil Scialli. They learned to trust our company secretaries, managers and employees for their repairs and paid their bills in a timely fashion. It was then and only then that my dad finally understood how his company made money.

Now take a deep look at your employer or group/division within your company and analyze exactly what your guys do to either make money or what is contributed to a much larger company to make it money. For example, you might be a claims adjuster that is part of a group within a larger company that sells auto insurance. Technically, the company itself makes money selling insurance policies, but you as the claims group make the company (or increase profits) by doing what? You need to find that out immediately, pinpoint it and become a major player in that area.

If we continue with that example, we might say that you realize that your claims department is responsible for analyzing claims, and make sure they are not fraudulent and the payouts are legitimate. So what can you do? You can sit there, day in and day out, processing claims as instructed or you can figure out how you can work harder, reorganize, refigure or any other thing you can think of that will speed up the claims process and better detect fraudulent claims. In turn, you will show your bosses, not by word only, but on paper, as to why they cannot stand the thought of losing you as an employee. Numbers don't lie, and if your hard work is quantified in profits for the company, then, in turn, your job is safely secure.

There are hundreds of examples one can give, but the key is to strip away the mundane tasks you are accustomed to at work and find out exactly what are the inner workings of your business.

In general, America has always found ways to simplify almost every job which dates back to the Industrial Age with Henry Ford and his invention of the assembly line. Ford was the father of the greatest System ever created, and every System today for every business is a derivative of that System. If you really think about it, we are just stuck in one big assembly line of life created by the large companies that minimize outward thinking and maximize redundancy in order to produce efficiently and maximize profits. It is only the forward-thinkers and the innovators who challenge corporate structure and find ways to improve their current company or go out on their own and become their own bosses.

Again let me repeat this for you one last time. This time I will say it in slang terms, "Figure out how your company makes money, be the best at doing it for them, then you got them by the balls. No need to let them know you got them by the balls, they already know. Trust me on this, and you will be compensated."

You must always remember that the sky is not always the limit for your salary within your company or group. There is a ceiling at which you reach that you can no longer go passed no matter how good you are. When you hit that barrier, you must decide to either make a career change or stay content at being the best at that job. Either decision is not a bad one, but staying sometimes breeds complacency, so be careful in not getting lazy.

We will touch further on knowing your own worth in upcoming chapters.

CHAPTER 6

Know Your "Stuff"

"There is no excuse for ignorance."

The System is purposely designed for getting what we call "idiots" to produce within it. Think about how many people you meet at any national retail store you walk into on a daily basis that you cannot figure out how they landed a job in the first place. How many times have you walked out of those stores saying to yourself, "How does that place make money with that person working there?" They do make money and lots of it. People who create Systems are the ones making the money, not the $8 per hour counterperson you just complained about. These Systems are developed so that those who refuse to want to learn and improve their lives and continue to remain ignorant always have a job available to them. It is this endless supply of cheap labor which keeps the revolving doors of corporate America

51

turning and profits at record highs. The only way to beat the System is to learn the System and acquire as much knowledge as possible within it to rise within its ranks.

This is probably my biggest pet peeve in the business world today: There are so many people who are absolutely clueless as to what they are talking about. Either they are people you work with, people on TV, people writing books or those in the pages of the newspaper—everyone has an opinion or something to say that they have no actual knowledge about. I like to just classify these people as "idiots," but that's not really the correct term because you are giving them an excuse not to be knowledgeable. An idiot cannot learn, while an ignorant person chooses not to. Ignorant people lack knowledge in the area they are discussing, and rather than keep their mouth shut and listen to others, they decide to make their opinions known without basis. When they continue speaking without any knowledge of a topic, the people listening quickly discredit them and the point they are trying to make. Once you lose respect from your colleagues and they deem you an "ignorant person," it is very hard to get that respect back. Sometimes, you never get it back. That is why it is so important to "Know Your Stuff."

In my first day of class in the third grade, I walked into the room and found the word written "Observe" on the chalkboard. I continued throughout my years of school to remember a few more quotes written on those boards, quotes such as "There Is No Excuse for Ignorance," and "Those Who Do Not Learn From History Are Doomed to Repeat It." If we look at these phrases, the tie that binds them is knowledge and retaining it.

Observe: Observing is one of the basic fundamentals of learning, and in order for you to know your stuff, you must be willing to observe and observe quietly. In Italian, we have an old

Neapolitan saying that goes, "*Il mistiere lo ruba con gli occhi*," which translates to "You Steal the Trade With Your Eyes." This saying is intended to tell you to observe your master tradesmen (or boss) with your eyes and learn by watching quietly. In watching alone, you can quickly learn the trade just by the way your boss acts and works, not necessarily by doing the work yourself. If you are too loud or act like a know-it-all upfront, you might intimidate your boss and they will never really want to teach you everything, keeping you as a laborer and never becoming a master tradesmen yourself.

Observing quietly, listening intently, and following instruction will help you build confidence in your superiors and they will slowly begin to relinquish some responsibility to you as time progresses. If you learn and get better, they will give you more to handle because you are making their job easier, and in turn, your stock in the company rises (and remember, like I said in previous chapters, if they don't keep working themselves, you will be replacing them in no time at all).

Observe anything and everything when working, and during that time period, ask lots of questions no matter how stupid you may think they are. Make sure to never ask the same question twice. Repeat questions will give the person who is giving you the answer a feeling that you are not listening and feel like their time is being wasted. If you are unsure about something, but you know it was already discussed, the best way to confirm if your memory is correct is to rephrase your question into a statement and see if the person agrees or corrects you. When they correct you in this manner, it gives them a sense that you are trying to learn and thus makes them feel important like a teacher and student dynamic.

Here is a basic example. Say you just started working for an architect and you ask the question: "What is the minimum thickness for an outside wall?" He tells you that four inches is the minimum. A few hours later, he leaves you to design a home and you need to draw the thickness of the outside wall, but you're unsure if he told you six or four inches. So, you go back to your boss and you can re-ask the same question or you can say, "I just wanted to confirm that six inches is the minimum wall thickness." He will quickly correct you and say no it is four inches and you can respond "Oh, that's right, I remember you said that. Great, let me get back to work." By answering in this manner, you are reconfirming your boss's knowledge and giving a sense of security that you are trying to learn your job.

"There is no excuse for ignorance:" Ignorance is the absence of knowledge, and in terms of business, there is no excuse for it. No matter what you do for a living, you need to be extremely knowledgeable of your job. This, again, is another basic fundamental of remaining employed and properly paid. How many people do you know who all they do is complain about their job and don't make enough money and so on and so forth. If they put that much energy into learning their job to the best of their ability, then they probably would be in a much better position. When you know your stuff—no matter what your stuff is—there is no argument a colleague, employer or a client can make to you without you having a legitimate rebuttal. It is this power that makes you an asset to your employer.

Knowledge is power!, and no one can take it away from you … no one! It is impossible to be knowledgeable in everything, so be selective as to where you invest your time. Being selective allows you to pinpoint exactly where you need improvement and hone your skills in order to maximize your earning potential. This will increase your success rate exponentially within your company, thus resulting in bigger paychecks.

It's much easier than you think to acquire knowledge in a specific area. First, you need to love what you are doing or be really excited about what you have been hired to do. If you do not love your job, you will never commit to getting better at it. No matter how hard you try to force yourself into learning it, your attention span will be easily affected, negatively affecting your retention rate, finally leaving you uninterested. The end result is getting fired shortly thereafter.

Second, pinpoint exactly what is it your job is fundamentally based on. When you wipe away all of the pomp and circumstance of your job title, what is it you really do for your company that makes them money (refer to this chapter later on in book)? Once you figured out what you really do, you need to completely immerse yourself in acquiring all the knowledge you can and as fast as possible. You start with books, magazine articles, guides, references, the Internet and any other source that will provide you with good reading material.

Reading plays a pivotal role to mastering your job. You must read, read and read some more. No matter how long you have been at a job, anything and everything that crosses your hands should be read. In this day and age where technology is continuously changing, you cannot rely on what you already know because you can find yourself on the outside looking in. Ask all the Baby Boomers who refused to accept computers in the 1980s. Today, everything is run by some type of computer as you read, author your own notes, guides, cheat sheets and store them in an easily accessible place for quick future reference. Reading and then re-writing the info in your own format allows your mind to process the information better, thus increasing your retention. I strongly recommend reading and then writing down notes, then reading these notes, and rewriting those notes into a simpler form. I have done this my entire life, and found it to be the best way of learning and retaining information.

Third, attend training and continuing education courses when made available, and when not available, ask your employer to make them available. No employer who truly understands business would hinder their employees from attending a course that would make them better at their job. In addition, these courses are a tax write-off for your employer. When attending these courses, continue to write and create your own manuals like you did when you read on your own. When your course is over, offer to teach or give your own course for your colleagues who did not attend the class. This will make you shine with your boss and earn you much respect among your colleagues.

Fourth, and probably the most important piece of eliminating your ignorance, is comprehension and application. In order to truly comprehend what you have learned, you must apply what you learned. As you learn new things, begin to implement them at work and see if they improve your work environment. Use logic, better known as "common sense" when and where to apply your new found knowledge. If you come out too strong and fall flat, you are assumed to be a know-it-all and the result is a lack of respect from your peers. If you come out too weak, you may come across as indecisive and no one will truly respect your business decisions.

You can usually introduce new ideas by making suggestions to your peers, instead of just telling them. Asking them permission to accept your suggestions is a passive-aggressive tactic with a high success rate. Start by applying new ideas on the small scale, making sure they stick, and become an accepted practice at work. The higher the success rate your early ideas have, the more you will become the "go-to guy" at that job, and in turn, your stock rises.

In the early stages, keeping it modest and remembering not to call out or embarrass any colleagues, especially the senior guys, will let you fly under the radar long enough to become such an important asset to your company that they will not be able to stand the thought of losing you to a competitor. Developing a reputation around the office as "The Guy Who Knows His Stuff" will make you an indispensable asset to the company. The System cannot function properly without smart people.

> **"Those who do not learn from history are doomed to repeat it!"**

Mr. Ahearn, my history teacher in high school, used the above saying to explain that if Adolf Hitler had done his research in history, he would never have decided to invade Russia during World War II because it had been Napoleon Bonaparte's doom some 100 years earlier. Fortunately for mankind, Hitler was no history buff and his attack on Russia quickly led to his demise. From the day I was introduced to that saying, it stuck with me the rest of my life, and through time, I simplified it to relate to life and not just history. My version is as follows:

> **"Those who do not learn from the mistakes of others are doomed to repeat those same mistakes themselves."**

A large part of knowing your stuff involves asking questions … lots of them. The funny thing is that there is no special formula on who to ask questions. You should ask anyone and everyone you come in contact with. Asking both personal and professional questions to various people you meet in life will help you mold your own life. It is not the questions that are important, but it is remembering the answers that makes it pivotal to your own success. Most importantly, listen and remember their stories of failure in life and at work. Learning where they went wrong will help you not repeat those same mistakes, almost guaranteeing you a shorter path to success. It doesn't matter if the person is or was a "Horse" or a "Boss" in life, or how rich or poor they are. Just listen and learn about their experiences. No book can teach you what the people around you can teach you just by listening to their stories.

In almost every story of success or failure, each person, at one point in their life, hit a fork in the road in which they chose for better or for worse. Most of these people failed to realize there was a "fork in the road" because they had no prior experiences to guide them. When they failed, it might not have been until years later that they realized it was a fork and failed to choose wisely. That's why it is imperative to learn from people to help you navigate through the many forks in your road you may be presented with.

Usually the lesser successful are the ones who are easier to approach to ask questions. They are more liberal in telling you their mistakes at work or in life, because many of them use their mistakes as excuses for their shortcomings. By remembering their mistakes, they just told you about, it assists you in steering clear of those pitfalls when they present themselves. The real key to success is not doing everything right (which is impossible), but limiting the wrong things you do. The only way to limit what you do wrong is to know your "stuff" ahead of time.

The fundamentals to knowing your stuff is **observing, learning** and **remembering**. By knowing your stuff, you will be guaranteed success at work, in business and in life.

Know Your Worth

*"God judges you by how good you are ...
bosses judge you by how much you get paid."*

D o you really know what you are worth? Around $1
million or so right? Maybe to your mom, wife or kids,
you are worth $1 million, but not in this context. The correct
question is "What is your worth in the System?" Many people
believe that their goal as an employee is to try to get as much
compensation as possible at all times. They also believe that
raises are mandatory just because they have been with a certain
company long enough without getting fired. Others make the
mistake of taking their salaries for granted and quickly find
themselves out of a job in a down market. That is why it is
important to know your worth at all times.

When you know your worth to your employer, you can develop a more clear vision of where you fall financially on the corporate ladder. It also provides you with an indicator of your own job security with that company. "How is that," you may ask? Take a look at what you get paid at your current job. You may already know where your pay lies with everyone else working in your particular company or group. If your pay scale is in the higher end of the salary spectrum, then your employment position and responsibilities should be in that same spectrum. If your salary grossly outweighs your actual skills, then you can be almost certain that when the axe falls, you will most likely be the first one on the chopping block.

"Knowing your worth" is a tool with immeasurable value to you as the employee. When you learn to grasp the value of your own contributions to the System, it becomes a giant bargaining chip in salary negotiations.

How do you determine exactly what you are worth to your company? The term "worth" does not need to be based solely on what your salary is compared to everyone else. There are other factors that come into play when determining your "worth," such as how hard you work for the company, how much business you bring in to the company, and how profitable you are to the company.

The first step in determining your worth is to actually break down your position at your company. What specific role do you play for your company? Compare it to how it contributes to the overall functionality of the company. No matter how mundane your job is, there is a specific value to it, or it wouldn't be a job. Determine your contributions and compare it to how your company makes money (as discussed in previous chapters) and

determine if your job is generating revenue c
enue (overhead) from the company.

For example, if you are working for an a
you are an accountant, then you are in a reve
sition. If you are working in human resources, then your position is part of the company's overhead. When you are considered
"Overhead," it means that your position is a required expense to
the company. It's a part of doing business which is paid from the
revenue-generating positions. Employees in revenue-generating
positions, with years of experience being equal, are better compensated than those in overhead positions.

Know that you have determined what role your job plays in
your company. The next thing to do is to find out how much
money others in the same industry with similar job descriptions
and duties get paid based on their tenure and experience. There
are various ways to find out what the going rate is for your type
of job. In large companies, it may consist of taking a walk to your
human resources department, sitting down with a human resources rep and asking for company data. They would usually
provide general data about the various positions within the company with a description of duties, titles, levels of experience and
various salary ranges. If you are in a small company or a company that does not disclose this type of data, and aside from your
typical "What are you making?" water cooler small talk, what
else can you do?

First and foremost, do not ask your colleagues what they get
paid! Your salary is your business alone, and their salary is their
business. Most of the time, colleagues will lie about their own
salary just to goad you into disclosing your own. Once you disclose the truth about your own salary, they will always find a

lem with it—especially if you are making more than them. Their jealousy will eat them from the inside, forcing themselves to compare every situation between you and them. It becomes an uncomfortable competition in which your every wrong move is amplified by jealous co-workers.

Therefore, if you cannot find the company salary information at the water cooler, then here are a few alternative methods. The Internet is a great source for researching salaries. In New York, for example, you can go to the NY Department of Labor's Web site and review actual wage statistics based on real salary data. These statistics give entry level, median and experienced salaries for specific occupations. Another method, and the most accurate form in finding the going rate for your position, is to interview with other companies similar to yours. It's a little dangerous to do because you don't want your company to find out and think you are jumping ship and are headed to the competition. However, by actually going out into the free market and sitting with other employers and listening to what they have to offer based upon your experience, you can easily gauge your actual worth in your own industry. If going on interviews is to risqué for you, then you can put the word out to persons like headhunters and see what sort of salaries they are offering. Even though using headhunters is not as accurate as actual interviews because you don't really see the way a company operates with your own eyes, it is still a quick way to find out what the market is offering in an incognito manner.

Okay, now that you have done your research on the range of salaries in your field, the next piece of data to find out is what the maximum possible salary a person can obtain in a particular position, no matter how much experience he or she accumulates. That is what we call the "ceiling" in business world. It is critical for anyone in gauging their worth to know what the "ceiling" is for their position. If you are in a position in a company in which there is no ceiling and the final destination is actual ownership, then that's great. Unfortunately, even at the ownership level, you need to figure out just what the ceiling salary is. If that ceiling salary is acceptable to your own personal standards of being an owner, then you know that there is room to grow and ownership is your ultimate goal.

All Systems and the levels within them have a ceiling, and as long as the ceiling is attainable and acceptable to the person trying to achieve it, then there are no major problems with employment. The problems arise, however, when you realize that your salary is very close or even worse, over, the ceiling salary for that particular position. Once you have determined the maximum salary you can earn at your position and realize that you already make that salary, then you must decide on one of two things. One, you can stay and accept the fact that this is what you will make do with for the rest of your employment except for minor wage increases to offset inflation. Or second, you can ask to change your current employment position to another position within your company with a higher ceiling salary. It is not as easy as I make it sound, because you need to prove to your superiors that you possess the skill set for a change of employment.

Through your own due diligence, you now posses the following pay data: Your current pay at your position based on your experience, the entry level pay, median level pay, experience level pay, and finally, the "ceiling" pay.

Now, let's analyze this data, using my own past experiences as an example. In 1997, I started working for approximately $32,000 a year, which was the entry-level salary at that time for a mechanical engineer. Throughout my years, I worked my butt off, to which I was rewarded with greater levels of responsibility at my position. Each year that passed, I received pretty good pay raises, somewhere in the 10% range annually. I really didn't make too much of the whole salary thing because I was fixated on immersing myself in their System and being the best at it. However, as time progressed, I realized that my production and profitability to the company was greater than my actual experience in years at the company.

Using the various techniques I explained in this chapter, I determined that my salary, after four years, was considerably lower than what the industry was mandating at the time based on comparable job duties. So, I asked for a meeting with my immediate boss, and then another meeting with the boss of the New York office at the time. He was a little man but tough as nails, and reminded me of Yoda from Stars Wars with an Indian accent. Most of the employees were scared to approach the guy for a raise, especially mid-year and six months away from actual reviews.

Instead, I never feared going into him, because I did my research beforehand. When I sat down in his office, I confidently asked for an adjustment to my salary, not a raise. I detailed to him how my work directly contributed to the company's profitability and that the level and quality of work I was producing was more comparable to an engineer with six years of experience, not four like me. In addition, I provided backup data, by naming and describing the projects, the work I performed and the profitability of those projects. Then, I used his own company salary and experience data against him by clearly identifying how much my salary should be adjusted upwards.

I knew that, at the time, the engineering employment market was hot, and my skill-set was commanding salaries in the $60,000-$80,000 range. So I didn't ask for $80,000 because I didn't want to be on the higher end of the scale, so I asked for $70,000. I knew that if the market cooled, my salary request wouldn't land me at the higher end of the spectrum, and also, my request didn't make me look like a hog. One week after my meeting with Yoda, I was awarded with a salary adjustment. I didn't worry during the week of waiting, I knew I was getting the raise, because "I knew my worth." I knew I was worth more to them than what they were paying me at the time.

In a future chapter, I will go into more detail on how to ask your boss for more money. Like the quotation states at the start of the chapter, you must realize that your boss gauges you by your salary and your salary only. Its basic math to them—an equation of how much you make for them, minus how much they pay you. If it is substantially lopsided in either direction, then each party can make a reasonable argument for an adjustment. Unfortunately, employers rarely ask employees to take a pay cut, they usually let you go. Employers do not believe in giving pay cuts because it leaves the employee disgruntled, which may lead to theft, a lack of production and/or both.

As I stated earlier in this chapter, it is imperative to always know your worth, and never live on the motto of "getting mine" alone. Trying to accumulate unwarranted high salaries solely for the purpose to make as much money as possible with total disregard of your actual intrinsic value to your employer will leave you jobless sooner rather than later.

So go ahead and do the research, see where you stand and make your adjustments as needed.

CHAPTER 8

Know Your Colleagues

"When you laugh, you laugh together. When you cry, you cry alone."

A good analogy can be made by comparing a business environment to a jungle in the literal sense. When in the System, it's survival of the fittest, with everyone having their eye on a specific prize. Nine times out of 10, that prize is more money, a bigger title, a better position and any other tangible asset someone may want in the company that they currently don't have. The American corporate system is purposely set up that way ... capitalism at its best! By making our corporate system a merit-type System, it forces each and every person in the company to go get theirs first before anyone else. With everyone trying to "get theirs," it, by default, activates one's human instincts to do whatever it takes to get theirs... no matter what.

For example, in extreme situations when you see totally peaceful people faced with major despair like an earthquake and food or water aid arrives late. The survival instincts of those in dire need will kick in to the point where they would trample those in front of them—including the aid workers trying to help them—to get to the water/food first.

That might sound extreme, but is it really? Our food/water source in the modern world has been supplemented by material things, but it triggers the same mechanisms in us to try to get them, no matter who we walk over or trample to get the prize. It is the reason why I strongly believe that you should know your colleagues. In order to be successful, you must analyze and study each and every one of the players in the System independently. Then, you must identify which of their traits will benefit you most at work, and which traits to steer clear of. Many individuals have the habit of classifying their colleagues, meaning their bosses, their vendors, their clients and their co-workers as friends, and get confused between respecting one another and friendships.

Respecting those you work with, and them respecting you, is not friendship: You need to see the distinction between the two. Basically, in a real friendship, a friend (family) can come into your life at any time and you can pick up just like you left off 10 years ago without skipping a beat. No matter what he or she says to you, what monies he or she has, your friend is there for you and you for them. For your friend, you will sacrifice all when asked to, and vice-versa. When you would rather let your own goals take a back seat to improving the goals of your friend, that represents true friendship.

At work, the dynamics of a so-called friendship are different. It is not an unselfish love for one another that keeps you together, but rather, a paycheck for getting a job done. When multiple people are trying to achieve the same goal, the result is competition. As I told you, there are no friends at work, I am also telling you that the words "friendly competition" cannot coexist either. No matter how mundane a task is, when two individuals are put in a situation to compete, it never turns out good for one of them. Why? Because one must win and one must lose; one must take credit for an achievement, and one will not. How many times at work do multiple people accomplish a task and the boss may only credit one person for accomplishing the task. In most instances, you will find that these once so-called "friends" are now at each other's throats?

Here is a simple question for you? How many BFFs do you have at work? If you have one, then you have too many. It is as simple as that. There are NO friends at work, and you should never have any! Early in my corporate career, I realized that a work environment was not conducive to friendships. In my first few months at the engineering firm, a firm comprised primarily of male employees, I could not believe the amount of whispering, backstabbing, complaining and whining amongst the employees regarding everything, especially amongst each other. I felt like these men were worse than a group of New Jersey housewives with a purse full of money at a hair salon. Everything from "This guy gets paid too much" to "This guy works too little" to "This guy's bonus was bigger than mine," and so forth. I was amazed at how catty these men were being to one another in a professional world. Then, it dawned on me that men are especially susceptible to this behavior because of our DNA.

Since the dawn of time, men have been programmed to be the "providers" in a patriarchal society, which meant to provide for their family at all costs. At an early age by emulating their own fathers (or any other patriarchal figure), they begin to learn and acquire this skill set to develop a fully mature "Alpha" mentality. The "Alpha Male" is a term used in describing any group or society of animals that live closely together and have a dominant leader. However, when they finally reach the corporate world, their Alpha Male mentality is abruptly met by many other Alpha Males with the same exact mentality. So what happens? That person will fall into one of three major categories:

1) **The Hyena:** Will lie, cheat, steal and scavenge their way up the ladder.
2) **The Jellyfish:** Will get ahead with no spine.
3) **The Wolf:** Will follow commands and accept the System, and wait for the opportunity to pounce.

Unfortunately, in the corporate world, there are a lot more Hyenas and Jellyfish than you think.

Beginning with The Hyena, the most common mistake made by the Alpha Male is to think that "pride" is a legitimate part of the Alpha mentality. Instead, their "pride" is a cancer that eats at them from the inside out, leading to jealousy, rage and any other unacceptable behavior that will get them fired by their superiors. How many times have you heard a colleague say, "I am not doing that … it is beneath me!" or "Nobody is telling me what to do! I know what I'm doing!" And then there is the best of all, "I don't get paid enough to do that."

These co-workers take starting at the bottom of the corporate ladder as an insult, believe work criticism is a personal assault on them, and generally feel they are underpaid the minute they walk in the door. Their pride gets them in trouble, and sooner or later, they start whining, complaining and sometimes worse. The "worse" can be backstabbing and colluding to bring you down with them. These co-workers are the rotten apples that spoil the bunch, and any good boss will sniff these types out and fire them in no time.

These Hyena types, and I have seen many in my day, will placate you to get what they want, and will do whatever it takes to get to the top with the least amount of work possible. Like real Hyenas, they will rather have someone do the work for them so that they can eat what is left. What they don't know is that the corporate cards are stacked against them and never does a colleague like this ever make it to the top. They are corporate bottom-feeders, moving from job to job, full of excuses and blaming others, with very little to show for it in their paychecks. They are scavengers who try to use the system to their benefit. These Hyenas are most common in the government, civil service and public school sectors. The reason why they flourish in these employment sectors is that they have the protection of laws and unions to guard their back, and terminating them is nearly impossible. So, they sit in the System, sucking the life out it until the whole System fails. Case in point, our school Systems.

C'mon! Don't be nervous ... you know exactly the type of person I'm talking about. Identify these Hyenas in your company, steer clear of them and never take their advice. Make sure you make them fully aware that your "kindness should never be thought of as weakness" and your coattails are not for riding on. Make these types of co-workers accountable for what they do, and don't let them slide, even if it means you picking up their slack for a particular task. Eventually, when enough time passes where they know they cannot intimidate you, they will quit on their own. Their own shortcomings, when compared to you, will become so apparent to your superiors that they will be fired or transferred.

The Jellyfish is probably the co-worker type I hate most of all. While The Hyena is pretty easy to identify, The Jellyfish is much harder to detect. They are the co-workers who seem to have the most friends, but bring the most trouble. How can this be? These people, much like a real jellyfish, have no spine. When they are with you, they are your best friend, and when they are with someone else, they are their best friend. They make you feel comfortable enough to discuss things you may not routinely speak about, like salary, bonuses, promotions, etc., They, in turn, tell you what you want to hear, so you divulge more and more about yourself and your plans. Little by little, they quietly get all the information they need about you and everybody else to stir enough proverbial pots in the office to create havoc. They are the ones who are in everyone's business, then purposely use some perfectly-timed information for their own benefit.

How many times in an office have you found yourself arguing with a co-worker you never argued with before only after you said something to someone else? That someone else is The Jellyfish. Their passive-aggressive nature gives the illusion of being harmless on the outside. Instead, they are highly-skilled manipulators who need to be identified when you are treading the corporate waters. Let's be clear. The Jellyfish is not your friend! They are the ones who call you at home to discuss work issues that necessarily are not about work. Instead, they rather dish the dirt about a colleague or a boss. To put it bluntly, I call them "Shit Stirrers." The common lines associated with them are, "Well, I don't want to get involved … but" or "You didn't hear this from me … but," or my favorite, "You know what I heard?"

Like the jellyfish, they live in all areas of the world, look beautiful and harmless, but pack a sting that may kill you. These co-workers coexist in all areas of the System and at all levels. Isn't it interesting that so many Jellyfish coexist in the corporate world for years without ever being fired?

Ironically, some bosses find them to be an asset. While not admitting it, bosses knowingly and wittingly use The Jellyfish to gather all the information they need on their employees. Even better, they use The Jellyfish to send out messages into the workforce without ever writing it on paper. As an employee of the same company, just make sure you only tell The Jellyfish what you want others to know, and that's it. Do not ever entertain their after-work calls or their after-hours socializing. Remember, you met these people at work. You have friends at home already and do not need any more.

The Wolf is the true Alpha and the best colleague to have around. The Wolf, like you, decided to join the pack (the company) and gives everything to the pack in order for the pack to survive and flourish. They will follow the commands of their boss to a tee, and put 100% effort in everything they are asked to do at all times. These Wolves have realized that talk is cheap and actions speak louder than words. They lead by example, and are usually the highest paid and most respected in any company, even by upper management.

All Wolves feel that, in every pack, the time will eventually come that their leader will step down and they will take over either quietly or forcibly. So, you might be asking, "If they are so great, why should I watch for them? Why can't they be my friends?" Well, these types of co-workers are not into friendships, they have one goal in mind, and that goal is being the lone Alpha Male. That means when the time comes and you are in the way of their ultimate goal, they will make it their mission to rub you out.

Wolves are fierce competitors with calculating minds, always trying to maximize their ability to be successful in their proverbial hunts and kills. They display a "right to the point" attitude about getting the job done at all costs. They don't want to be friends with you. They want you to work for the benefit of the team. They don't let you slide, hold you accountable and make it a point to find your weaknesses so they can expose them at the right time. Like the real wolf, this type of Wolf stalks its prey and attacks when its probability of success is at its greatest.

That's why I love The Wolf, and as long as you identify who these co-workers are, then they can be great team players. The key is to never show them weakness when dealing with them, always bring your "A-Game" to the table, and never back down from a competition, task, confrontation or situation. Any time there is something at stake, you need to remind The Wolf that you are ready to sacrifice just as much as them to get it. If done correctly with respect and integrity, a mutual admiration will develop for one another, a respect that will result in the strongest and most profitable unit in the company. The key is to know that, one day, no matter how strong the bond may be, one of you will have to stake claim to full Alpha Male status.

CHAPTER 9

Asking For More Money

"Set the example ... don't be the example."

Three years into my tenure at the engineering firm, we were hired for the MEP (mechanical/electrical/plumbing) systems design for a new children's hospital being built in New York. This was a ground up project, and was considered a large project even for our company, a project that had consulting fees in the hundreds of thousands of dollars. I was roughly making around $45,000 a year and was put in charge of designing both the fire protection and medical gas systems. My associate Bill was in charge of the remaining plumbing systems design for the same project. Bill had been in the business about 20 years already, and had worked for various companies during his time as a consultant. He was a great guy, but Bill was definitely a "Horse" and not a "Boss." He simply wanted his day's pay and nothing more. So when another opportunity came knocking midstream of our hospital project, Bill went for the bigger paycheck and left our company for the second time in his career. With this huge project still in need of completion, my boss left it to me to get it finished by the deadline.

About a month or two after Bill's departure, I remember sitting at my desk, seething over the fact that I was being paid so little in contrast to being responsible for so much. They had a three-year engineer (me) with a salary to match, designing something routinely done by engineers with three times both the experience and pay. It wasn't that I couldn't handle the technical end of the job. Being the son of plumber and a mechanical engineer, in my own right, designing this stuff was second nature to me. Nor was it the actual workload (meaning man hours) that bothered me either. I had that work ethic that my parents had taught me, so I did everything I had to do to get it done for the deadline. Working at the office late, logging in remotely from home, or coming in on Saturdays to pick up the extra workload was routine for me.

My discord actually stemmed from the fact that I knew that my skills were special and they were using my three years of professional experience as a reason to underpay me my true worth. In other words, they knew that an engineer with my experience was only worth so much in the free market, so they didn't care if they had a guy who was as qualified as one with 10 years under their belt.

So, being immature at the time, I would sit there and complain out loud to anybody who would listen to my rift with management. Most of them could care less, because they weren't friends who cared. They figured if I was getting less, then there was room for them to get more. However, one day, another colleague of mine, Rich, walked into my office and asked me what my problem was? It was that five-minute conversation with Rich that taught me one of my greatest lessons to date in business.

Rich was a straight-shooter, "a Horse", and had much more experience in navigating the corporate System than myself at the time. His honesty, coupled with his experience, was a valuable asset to me, and I valued his opinion greatly. So it was important to me that he heard me clearly state my case about deserving more money in my paycheck. After a few minutes stating my case, he said to me, "What are you going to do about it?"

"That's easy," I said to him. "I'm going to walk into my manager's office, sit down at his desk and tell him I deserve more money!"

Without skipping a beat, Rich asks, "Why do you deserve more money?"

"Well, when Bill was here, we both had two major parts to the hospital project," I replied. "And when Bill left the company, his workload was dumped on my lap to finish. Did they hire someone else? Nope. Instead, I did my work... and Bill's work too! That's why I deserve it!"

Rich, with a small smirk, asked one very simple question, "Are you doing a good job?"

I almost didn't want to answer him. The mere thought of not doing a good job was out of the question, and he knew exactly how anal I was with my designs. But I turned and said, "Of course it's not a good job, it is a great job! I'm the best and you know it Rich!"

"Yeah, yeah ... are you done listening to yourself speak?" Rich said jokingly.

"Now let me teach you something before you make an ass out of yourself with the boss," said Rich. "Sometimes, things that seem so clear to you are not what they seem when seeing it through the eyes of the boss."

I didn't understand what he was trying to tell me, so he continued.

"When you tell your boss about how great you are and how wonderful an employee you must be for picking up the slack from Bill's departure and doing it with ease, your boss is not going to give you a raise, but might demote you instead," remarked Rich.

"What? Are you crazy?" I rebutted.

"No, I'm not crazy," replied Rich. "It is basic math my friend. Your boss looks at what you are telling him in a totally different manner than you. He sees that you and Bill worked together for three years comfortably doing the work. Then when he left, you were doing both his work and yours with no problem. Not only did you do it, but you did extremely well by your own admission. So if his math is correct, you were only working at 50% capacity for the first three years at the company. Only after Bill's recent departure did you finally work at your full potential. Therefore, you will owe your boss back half of your salary for the past three years. Resulting in a demotion instead of raise! How do you like them apples?"

You know he was the only one laughing. I was left speechless, because Rich taught me a huge lesson on how to ask for more money. He showed me the view from the perspective of the boss, a perspective that made more sense the more I thought about it. All along, I was thinking that the points to my argument were bullet-proof, but instead, they were all the ammunition my boss needed to get me demoted.

If you didn't get it, go back and read the story until the point of the boss's argument is crystal clear to you. When asking for money, one major thing to remember is to see your boss's view of you asking him. This will allow you to play out all the scenarios that may arise at the bargaining table before you get to it. Role-playing the scenario at home, with a family member acting as you and you acting as your boss is an invaluable tool. This role-playing mechanism will help you build self-confidence and allow you to formulate responses to any and every situation that may or may not arise during the raise request process.

When asking for more money, it is pivotal that you ask with confidence, no shakiness in the voice and look clearly at your boss in the eye. As discussed earlier in Chapter 7: Know Your Worth, you must clearly identify to your boss how you are an asset to their company. With the confidence of speaking at hand and the ammunition of "knowing your worth," let us go through the important steps you must take, and more importantly, what steps not to take when properly asking for a raise. This is just a reminder before you move forward. You must truly know your worth and determine that it is undervalued when asking for a raise. If this is not the case, then don't even continue reading because it's not going to work.

The first thing to do is to identify who the boss is within the System. That, for some, is easy because you work for one guy who is your boss and he also owns the company. However, it is not so easy in some larger companies. These companies have multiple bureaucratic layers in which the boss you currently report to is not the actual guy who signs off on your raise. If this is the case in your company, then you must go through the process of identifying who the money person is and if a meeting can be set directly with them.

There is no reason to prepare yourself to go speak to an immediate boss who is going to turn around and tell you, "I will have to go to management and I will let you know what they say." It's a waste of time, and most of all, nobody is ever going to go to bat for you as you would for yourself. In my own personal experiences, my immediate boss never ever came back with good news from management. Their typical response would be, "Management appreciates your hard work, but ..." Remember, your immediate boss will hesitate to push hard for your raise because they do not want to piss off the same people who are also going to give them a raise.

The question then arises, "Just what do you do?" If you have corporate layers to go through, then start at the closest layer first and recruit them in your pursuit to getting a raise. Go to your immediate boss and tell them about your intentions of wanting more money, and ask them for their assistance in getting you this raise. By inviting them in, you will not alienate yourself by going directly over their head. In addition, since they have the most immediate impact on you and you on them, this recommendation carries the heaviest weight with upper management.

The key is to tell your boss that you want a meeting with upper management and you want them to be present when you go. If they offer to do it alone for you, tell them that if they fail at getting you the pay raise, then you are going to go directly to their superior to find out why. Most often than not, they will opt to go in with you and not go in alone. This will spare them the embarrassment of failing you and the embarrassment with management when you go over their head anyway. It will make them look ineffective as a boss. Putting your immediate boss on the spot is the best position to have them in, because at the meeting, there is no misunderstanding as to what is being said. When all discussions are open to all parties, it eliminates the "telephone game" which is the misinterpretations that routinely occur from one conversation to another.

Timing is a second key … knowing when to ask for your raise. If you leave it up to your boss, asking for more money is never a good time. That is why it is important for you to take the initiative with your boss to meet. The term "ask" is key to understanding. If you think by complaining under your breath to other colleagues and making waves large enough so that your boss has become aware that you are disgruntled over salary is defined as "asking," then you are way off the mark. Unfortunately, this is all too common in the corporate world. Employees are scared to directly ask for a review, so instead, they resort to complaining which has a success rate of "very limited" to "nothing at all." It is actually more of an annoyance which disrupts the team and can result in an early termination rather than promotion.

If you have a boss/owner scenario where there are no set dates for reviews and raises, then it is important that you take the first step in setting up a review process with them first. Approach your boss and ask them for a time to review your job and salary one on one, preferably after hours where disturbances are at a minimum. Make sure you tell them that you want the review, months from the day you ask, but not longer than one year. Asking for an immediate review will make you look like you are out for their money only and are far removed from being a team player. By setting the review date far in advance, your boss cannot make excuses not to make time for you. If you just started your employment and you are confident in your abilities to succeed at your job, then set up your review date immediately. This is the starting point at which you will need to get the ball rolling.

If your company's System has a standard review date set, then never ever go and ask for more money between review periods.

Never request this, no matter how much you think you deserve it. Asking between periods breaks team unity and goes against corporate structure. This will make you look selfish to both your bosses and your peers.

Every year, request your review and agree on some type of salary terms for the job you are doing. This is somewhat of an informal contractual agreement until the next review. Just like when your favorite professional athlete decides to renegotiate their contract during the current season, how does it make you feel? It's the same feeling your bosses and colleagues get when you go ask for a raise in between reviews. You may have legitimate reasons for wanting and deserving one, but you will have to suck it up and wait for your next review.

It is also imperative you never set up this review during your company's slow season or on a down year. Unfortunately, every industry has a down period, including yours. You need to find out what time of year your company is slow and steer clear of those time periods for asking for more money. The morale of management, along with corporate bank accounts, are very low during this time, and asking for a pay increase will make you look inconsiderate to the team.

If you are in a down year, in which a recessive economy has directly impacted the company, then the problem is much larger. Again, you cannot ask for a raise during this time, but unfortunately, this recession might last much longer than one could anticipate. During these times, management is looking to cut jobs and work longer hours for those individuals they keep. If you are one of those individuals whom they keep employed, do not get confused in thinking the extra workload is a prerequisite for a raise. Instead, just be happy that you are working because believe it or not, a bad economy works to your employer's advantage.

Bad economies purge once good employees, employees who may be overpaid, and dump them back into the job market. The employee pool becomes much larger and the options for your bosses grows by the day. This allows them to replace you or anyone else with the same skill set or better at a cheaper rate. It is amazing how the outlook of a once defiant employee changes when they have been jobless for a few months and the bills are stacking up. A word to the wise … never ask for a pay increase during a bad economy.

Okay, let us say that the timing is perfect, and that you are granted your review meeting. Now its time to prepare for the meeting and what is to take place at this meeting. The first thing you need to work on is your physical appearance and presentation when going into the meeting. I believe that you should go into your review with the same attire that you wear on a regular basis to work. If you overdress, you look like you are putting on a show simply for monetary gain. It's a fake approach and is easily read by your bosses. If you come underdressed, then that's another clear sign that you simply do not care for the job, and it shows a lack of respect towards your boss and their company. This is not a fashion show nor a popularity contest, it is your job, so respect it as if you were going to church. In general, women should try to keep the attire professional and avoid sexiness. The latter will cheapen your argument for deserving a raise.

Regardless of your attire, you must attend your meeting with a kept haircut, cleanly shaven, breath smelling fresh, teeth brushed and unscented deodorant. Cologne or perfume is optional, but never too much where it can become a distraction. Don't put lots of jewelry on display either. Other than the basics like a watch for a man and earrings for a woman, too much jewelry gives the presumption that the raise is going for vanity items. If you choose to wear a watch, make sure your watch is never more in value than the watch your boss is wearing. Men especially tend to look at watches, similar to women who may look to compare purses and/or shoes. Tattoos and any other personal statements should be covered before the meeting.

At the meeting, when you walk in, immediately shake hands. They are probably standing to greet you, so wait for them to tell you to take a seat or sit down when they take their seat first. This will immediately let them feel as if they are in control of the situation, and will ease any combative tensions that may exist. By acting submissive, but not in a kiss-ass way, will allow your boss to think they are running the meeting, even though you were the one who initiated it in the first place.

Don't bring papers, briefcases, presentation boards, etc., to the meeting. It is not a show. You and only you is all that is needed to state your case for a raise. If its warranted, trust me, your boss already knows why you are there and called for the meeting. This meeting, in general, is just to determine how much you really want and how much they are willing to give you in return. It's a negotiation, so there is no need to be nervous. Your chances are already in your favor or you wouldn't be sitting there in the first place.

When you sit down, look relaxed and don't cross your arms. Your boss will likely initiate the conversation about how the both of you got to this meeting. Hopefully, it was done in a professional manner and you didn't do it through complaining to others. Small talk will often begin the meeting, small talk that may concern your family or the previous night's local sporting events. Keep the answers just what they are … "small talk." Avoid long-winded life stories because your boss truthfully does not care. You just need to break the ice before getting to the point. Once the small talk is out of the way, they will begin asking you, in a nutshell, as to why you are there and it is at this point where you begin to take over.

Remember, go through practice exercises at home, and clearly state your case to your boss. You know your worth, so make them see the same. How you do it, in the next five minutes, is completely up to you and your style. All I can recommend is that while you are speaking, you need to keep a straight eye on your boss and play off of them and any reads you might be getting from them. Remember that getting a raise is only acceptable when your worth to your company outweighs what they are paying you and nothing else. All other reasons for getting a raise should never be brought up. The following three are the most common reasons used and have short-term success rates if any.

1. The Mercenary: This reason is commonly used during good times in a busy economy. This is when you defend getting a raise by telling your boss that you can get or have been offered more money elsewhere. If the boss does not give the raise you are requesting, then you are pretty much going to quit and go somewhere else. By putting a gun to their head and handing them an ultimatum, only one of two things is going to happen. They will call your bluff and ask you to take your stuff and leave right now, or will reluctantly give you the raise, but knowingly put you in their sights to get rid of you the minute they have an opportunity to do so.

This style of getting a raise makes you look like a mercenary because you are in it solely for the money. This shows blatant disloyalty to your company and exudes selfishness. This style may work a few times, however, your reputation will precede you and it will be increasingly difficult to get rehired. These types of employees are the ones who show up with super-long resumes showing short stints from company to company. This style works in good times, and can get you paid quickly, but if you don't back it up with true worth, your new company will hand you your walking papers just as quick. Trust me, if you like your work environment and the people, don't attempt this tactic to try getting a raise. You may find yourself working in a totally different company for a few more dollars, but miserable as well. If you are into burning bridges, then "The Mercenary" approach is right up your alley.

The exception to using this style is if the other offer is so large that your boss refuses to come close. Or, if you have fulfilled everything asked of you to get a raise, your boss has left you no other option to do so.

2. The Struggle: Never legitimize you getting a raise based on the struggles you have at home or outside of work. You don't deserve more money at work because things are tough at home. What you fail to realize is that everyone has problems, no matter where you fall on the corporate ladder. Unfortunately, bad times do not discriminate, and you have no clue what your boss is going through in their own personal life. What is personal should remain personal and should have no bearing on what goes on in the workplace.

In addition, using "The Struggle" style actually does an injustice to you because it cheapens your worth at work. If you are asking for a raise because of a situation in your personal life, then you never show your boss what you are really worth to their company. All they are thinking is that they likely have another charity case on their hands. Money on merit is what you want, not money on charity. Now don't get me wrong, there are some legitimate struggles that one might get confronted with and that is where you can maybe ask for financial help in resolving a particular issue with somewhat of a guarantee of paying it back. But that's not a raise.

Remember to think like your boss. If you give them the whole "struggle" story, all it does is remind them of their own "Nobody helped them get to where they are now" story. I know you have heard that story many times from at least one of your bosses. True or not, they always feel like they are where they are today based on hard work and dedication alone. That is the only way to also approach them. By using "The Struggle" technique on them, it makes them feel uncomfortable. Similar to when a homeless person asks you for a quarter on the streets, it makes you uncomfortable. We all have problems, so forget using your "struggle" story for getting a raise.

3. The Comparison: I bet you already have a feeling about what this one is about. This is when you tell your boss that you deserve a raise because you are a better worker than another colleague. Or, someone else got a raise, so you deserve one as well. Why in the world would you justify your worth by gauging it against another employee? Your worth is based solely on your own contribution to your company … period. The easiest way for your boss to diffuse this argument is to compare you to a superior co-worker in lieu of a deficient one. Now that the tables are turned against you, you truly lack a concrete basis for your argument.

Most people who present this "Comparison" argument to their bosses always choose an employee they know they are better than, but never complain when an employee who is better than them get a raise. This comparison style causes all sorts of problems in a company's employment structure, and it snowballs into fighting amongst employees and reduces the strength of the unit, resulting in a decrease in production. Bosses hate when you compare yourself to someone else, because you are telling them that they are not good at their jobs. Their sole purpose as a boss is to identify the correct person for that position to maximize profitability. So when you start with your "better than him and her" argument, you are telling your boss that they have no grasp on their employees and company. Most of the time, this is untrue. Good bosses know the exact pros and cons of each of their employees, including you. Don't worry about the guy next to you, just worry about yourself. Once your colleagues find out that you thought you were better than them (and usually the boss is the one to spill the beans), your life at work will become increasingly miserable.

"So set the example, don't be the example."

Finally, with the review coming to a wrap, your boss is either going to give you a raise on the spot, deny you the raise, or tell you to wait for a specified time. If you got the raise on the spot, then congratulations, and make sure you live up to those expectations that you promised to deliver and beyond.

If you were denied the raise, then thank them for the opportunity to discuss your salary and ask for a set of criteria that you will need to meet in order to get a pay increase down the line. If they provide this criteria, then ask them for another review date to discuss these achievement and milestones so that it is documented on the review. This will hold the feet of your boss to the fire just as much it is your responsibility to fulfill their wishes and expectations of you as an employee.

If your boss gives no real reason for not giving you the raise, or if the criteria presented is unattainable, then it is okay to start looking and preparing to find another place of employment.

However, most of the time, if you truly asked for your worth and not more than that, your boss will be honest enough on what they want you to achieve for a bigger paycheck. If they ask you to wait for a later time, and they have been truthful with you before, then wait it out like a man and continue working hard while showing that you are committed. Make sure that the time period agreed upon to meet down the line is an actual date and not a general unknown date. If you leave your review meeting in limbo, then you too will most likely remain in limbo. If you get the feeling they are blowing smoke up your ass, or they have done this to you before, then they are the one actually not being the team player, and in turn, there is nothing wrong with finding employment elsewhere.

Hopefully, this chapter has given you a clear and distinct road map to asking for more money, and if navigated successfully, should produce some rewarding results. I look forward to hearing some of your own experiences in asking for more money, so keep me posted.

CHAPTER 10

A Little Brooklyn In Business

"Everybody's got a plan ... till you get punched in the mouth."

O
f all the chapters I have written, this chapter will most likely be the most misunderstood and misinterpreted by readers. The reason why? This chapter asks something different of you, which may or may not be in your makeup as a person. It is something more intrinsic to the individual, and it really cannot be taught. By analyzing the anatomy of what it means to be "Brooklyn," you will see how it directly correlates to the business world.

When you think of "Brooklyn," what do you think of? Yeah, I'm talking about Brooklyn, N.Y. You gotta a problem "wit dat!" I don't care what part of the world you are from, you can pick out a Brooklynite from a group of people within seconds of speaking to them. Is it the accent? Very distinguishable, but Fugehdattaboutit! Is it the wardrobe? You mean the blue Yankee hat worn with every possible piece of wardrobe ensemble. Is it the nationality? Not every Brooklynite is a hairy-chested Italian named Tony, wearing a wife beater, velour suit and white sneakers. So what is it about Brooklyn that makes it so special? Well it's not the actual geographical Brooklyn that I am talking about, but rather, the proverbial "Brooklyn" is what I would like to discuss.

Being "Brooklyn" and being from Brooklyn are two totally different things. Being "Brooklyn" is that strong-willed, straight to point and intimidating presence you feel when you are with a true Brooklynite. They are generally loud, boisterous and tell you exactly how they are feeling at that exact moment, no matter whose feelings may get hurt. They have inherent street smarts that makes them less susceptible to scam artists. Sometimes, it is their superior street smarts that makes it easy for them to prey on the unknowing and the trustworthy. They carry a certain swagger with them no matter where they are. They make no excuses for who they are, and are proud of it. It is this type of "all about me" attitude that being "Brooklyn" is all about.

It's funny how many times I have met people in my life, and was automatically pegged as Brooklynite. In actuality, I probably spent more time shaving in my life than actually in Brooklyn. However, while most people may be insulted for being associated with such a so-called "crass" bunch, I actually take it as a compliment. The reason why it's a compliment is that, when properly used, this particular style and swagger can reap one many benefits. For me personally, it's an actual switch that I like to turn on, at any time, no matter who is present, to get whatever I want or get whatever point across that I want to at that particular time.

Like an actor entering a grand stage with all of the lights on them, the "Brooklyn Show" begins much the same way.

When we dissect being "Brooklyn" to its barest essentials. It is made up of two distinct traits: Intimidation and Attitude. No matter who you are, where you are from, and what you are, you posses these same two basic traits. The difference between you and the Brooklynite is that these traits maybe buried deep inside you and can only be triggered by alcohol or anger. Instead, for the Brooklynite, they are right at home with these traits and these traits serve as the foundation of their persona. Remember, being "Brooklyn" is a selfish persona created with its sole purpose to benefit you no matter what situation arises. That is why it should be used in moderation at select times, and not adapted as an everyday style. Projecting this style continuously would be overbearing for any work environment, and would most likely leave you without a job.

All leaders, winners and successful people who you work with or work for possess some piece of "Brooklyn." If you don't think so, try this experiment with your boss (do it only if you have a good enough relationship). Go into their office and attack the company, their leadership, or their own work. Whatever it is, just attack the work and don't attack them personally. Within minutes, or maybe even seconds, you will get them red hot under the collar, leaving you just short of being fired. Why do they get to this level of hot-headedness? Very simple ... because successful people care. That's right ... they care about their jobs so much that they take the attack as if it were on them personally. They forget to distinguish between the "job" and the "person." Therefore, when you attack the work, it is like attacking them, or even worse, their kids. They will fight you to the death to protect it. That's when their inner "Brooklyn" comes out full force. It is always funny to see a usually reserved boss get triggered to the point of dropping F-Bombs at twice the rate of a rap video.

Intimidation

There are two parts to intimidation. The first part is "dealing with intimidation" and the second part is "being the intimidator." In any business, at one time or another, you are going to deal with a colleague, boss or client trying to intimidate you for their benefit. Basically, they will be out to make you the example for their own gain at work. Intimidation generally occurs when you are new to something, where a superior or colleague feels they have an opportunity to feel you out. They will see what you are made of, and how far or hard they can push you before you reach a breaking point. It is called "The Line," and we all have one. It is your job to make The Line so wide and that you cannot be pushed over it. Make The Line too thin and nobody will want to work with you. The Line you define is what everyone around you will learn to live by. Therefore, it is imperative to have flexibility when setting your limits.

For example, when I worked at the engineering firm, I made it clear that there was a time for work and a time for play and no in-between. When I was in so-called "Work Mode," I made sure that me and those around me were producing and not goofing off. I made sure that people were held accountable and excuses were not acceptable. I was a team player and never believed in that whole blame game or throwing your co-workers under the bus technique for personal gain. When I was thrown under the bus, I made it clear to the person who committed the offense that the terms of the relationship would have to change. They were fair game, and their work and actions would be under the utmost scrutiny. I gave respect and expected the same respect in return. When I felt that the reciprocation was not there, I made sure I dealt with that individual, no matter their position.

When dealing with intimidation, you need to first ascertain if the intimidation is "direct" or "indirect." The "direct" type of intimidation is the easiest to notice, but the most difficult to deal with because it usually consists of an "in your face" confrontation. When this situation occurs, you need to identify that it is happening, and immediately need to decide your course of action. If you do nothing, then you may leave yourself open to future situations. If you decide to stand up to the aggressor, then you need to be prepared to fight (literally and figuratively) for your respect. At that moment, you need to show that you are just as serious to take it to the next level as the person who is attempting to intimidate you. Think of it like a playing a game of Texas Hold 'Em and the chip leader is betting heavy, waiting for you to fold. Do you fold or call their bluff, and see what cards they are holding? Sometimes by calling their bluff, you test the intimidators' mettle, and the end result is usually a mutual respect of one another.

The key to the situation is to know exactly how much are you willing to risk to earn your respect and how far to let it escalate. At some point, you might have to jeopardize your own employment by actually showing that the job itself is secondary to proving your point. In other words, you would rather get fired than be intimidated by someone else. This approach is so against the corporate grain that people are left to wonder what the hell you are actually thinking in that situation. More often than not, this "Brooklyn" approach leads to a back down of the aggressor and cooler heads will prevail.

When being intimidated, one should never let a situation escalate to actual physical violence, especially in the business environment. At no time do I condone actual physical violence towards another person. I have been in numerous situations where things were escalating rapidly and I would tell the person, "Listen, let's argue the situation, but there is no reason for being disrespectful. I don't talk to you in that manner, so please don't talk to me in that manner. If you continue on like this, we are going to have a personal problem instead of a business issue." This is telling the person you can agree to disagree without being unprofessional. The person usually realizes they are out of line and their tone changes. However, men will sometimes be men and "a good shot to someone's big mouth" might make an unreasonable person get straight quick. Like Mike Tyson said, "Everybody's got a plan," and the key is to make sure to let everybody know that their plan may not be your plan at that time.

The "indirect" type of intimidation is probably the one I hate most in business. It's the individuals at work who would rather go to a superior about something than confront you directly. You know exactly which ones I'm talking about. They are the "reporters" who report everything back to the boss, looking for any way to make you look bad for their own gain. I dub this type the "shit talkers."

Since these types are passively aggressive and usually hate confrontation, they are the easiest to deal with. When you feel a situation occurring, the easiest scenario is to nip it in the bud right then and there. Go straight to the source, aka the "shit talker," and ask to speak with them in private immediately. In private is best done when you are dealing with a first-time offender. If the person happens to be a repeat offender, then you call them out no matter where they are.

Calling someone out in the open is the best form of being "Brooklyn." It's the public stage where you can address everyone at once about a particular situation. A public forum as such not only addresses that specific person, but it's direct as well. You put everybody else around you on notice as well. When you pull the big show, you better be very particular on what you are saying and who the audience is. It is imperative to remember that whatever comes out of your mouth at that moment cannot be taken back. This technique is the most effective and also the most risky. When properly done, your co-workers will think twice before doing something that might directly affect you or your job. In other words, the "shit talker" will shit their pants!

If you are hesitant about calling someone out in the open, but would like to still address a situation but not one-on-one, then the next best thing is to call a meeting with you, the "shit talker" and the boss. By going to the boss, it cannot be done in a whiny, cry baby-type manner, but rather, in an assertive fashion. You need to tell your boss why you asked for the meeting, and then identify the problem you are having with the person and what they are saying. Make sure your argument rebuts that person's statements, and finally, tell your boss that you will not stand for this if it continues or happens again.

If you are a good employee, and there is strong merit to your argument, your boss will definitely put that employee on notice, reminding them that if the problem persists, they will have to answer to them instead of you. This assertive style may prove to have another added benefit. Being assertive will show leadership to your boss, and leadership, coupled with a legitimate argument made by you, will convince the boss that you have the company's best interests in mind and can handle any precarious situation with professionalism. This approach can be a win/win situation for you.

Being the Intimidator

If I have to explain to you what this means, then you are probably going to have a very difficult time grasping the concept of being one. In the business world, you will be put in situations where you may have to intimidate a boss, a client or a colleague for your own personal gain. Like I wrote earlier, intimidation is usually done from higher ups to those below them on the corporate ladder, but that is not always the case. Therefore, your first attempt at intimidation will most likely be with a co-worker at the same level as you or maybe at a lower level in the company. Honestly, it really doesn't matter, as long as you go "Brooklyn" at the right time to maximize your benefit.

When being the intimidator, you need to determine a few things upfront. The first thing is to determine the type of intimidation you are attempting: Authoritative, Intellectual or Physical Intimidation?

"Authoritative Intimidation" is testing the boundaries of just how much you can really get away with at your position of authority. Just how intimidating can you be based on the power you possess? Can you fire the person you are going to intimidate? The power you have will most likely gauge the effectiveness of your intimidation.

"Intellectual Intimidation" is being smarter or better at your job than others. This type of intimidation is usually effective for those who lack the authoritative power to do so. In this case, you intimidate your co-workers by just being better than them at their own job. This means that no matter what they do or say, they can never give you an excuse for something because you can do it or know it better than them. Personally, I love this form of intimidation the most. When you know exactly what you are talking about, people will never second guess your decisions. If they try to second guess you, then you can break them down in so many different ways as to why they are wrong in their assessment that they will fear doing it ever again (this has a direct correlation to Chapter VI: Know Your Stuff).

"Physical Intimidation" is pretty self-explanatory. This requires using your physical size or reputation to get your point across without actually getting physical. This method works best for larger and more imposing persons for obvious reasons. However, even individuals who are known to have a reputation of not backing down from confrontation like a Brooklynite can also have the same effect. Race, nationality, sex, stereotypes and reputation are all different types of factors that can play a role in Physical Intimidation.

At an early age, I realized how some of my African-Americans friends used their race to intimidate others based on stereotypes. These guys were sweethearts, but when we were playing a predominately white school in football, they would put on a show better than Ringling Brothers! Mentally, they had already won the football game before it even started. I learned a lot from those friends, and in business, I have used and continue to use my Italian heritage and the associated stereotypes to play into people based on what they want to see or hear at that time and moment.

Using Physical Intimidation is a dangerous gamble and needs to be done at a time and place where your other two options will not work alone. Physical intimidation, if performed incorrectly, can be misconstrued as a threat of violence in the workplace. To threaten someone is not the intention of the intimidation. The true intent of intimidation is to make sure that the people understand the arguing of facts and nothing else. If they veer off in another direction with their arguments, their chances of winning are greatly reduced.

In other words, it is like when the United States brings an aircraft carrier into a region of conflict like North Korea. They are telling the world, "You can argue, but don't flex because we are the big dogs here." That's what Physical Intimidation is all about. A physical presence is immediate so you don't have to even explain yourself. People see your size or have heard stories of your reputation and already have it in their heads before even saying a word. Having this in your arsenal already gives you a huge advantage in the workforce, so it is important not to abuse it.

Authoritative, Intellectual or Physical Intimidation can be used individually or together. It is my opinion that together, they are much more effective than if used individually.

The second thing is to predetermine your reason for intimidation before doing it. For example, here is a list of few instances when to exercise intimidation:

1. To teach someone a lesson. Make them an example.
2. To get your point across to someone or a group.
3. To gauge a person's "line," meaning how much can that person take.
4. To showcase yourself to a boss, colleague or client.

Make sure you know exactly why you are doing something before you do it. Also, play out the scenario in your head so that you are ready for any reaction you may receive from the person you are intimidating.

The final thing is to make a mental notation of the success rate of your intimidation. Did it work to your advantage? Did you accomplish what you set out to do? Did you make matters worse for yourself? Intimidation takes lots of practice, especially if you are not that type of person to begin with. However, it is like a drug, the better you get at it, the more you want to do it. It is very important to remember that overuse of any kind of intimidation makes you a bully and that is not the intention of this chapter. Just remember that if you think you can be a financial success in business without intimidation, it will never happen. It is weaved into the capitalistic fabric of our society.

"Attitude" is the final component to business success, no matter whether you believe it or not. Many people find or see successful people as cocky, arrogant, conceited and slightly narcissistic. That may be a fair judgment of character for some; however, I believe that most successful people began their journey with drive, attitude and a sheer determination to achieving their goals. This drive may sometimes appear to others as the negative traits described, but in reality, those individuals are not what they seem to be. Their focus on personal success obscures them from being the so-called "nice person" you want them to be.

There are times when I can walk through an entire office of people and not say hello to any of them. It is not because I want to. Instead, I'm not really seeing them mentally at that time. I'm focused or thinking of a job at hand and don't really hear or see what is directly in front of me. In other words, it is like my brain shuts down for the mundane to focus on what is important at that given time. That focus is what many call an "attitude," but more in a negative way. Don't get me wrong ... I strongly feel that prolonged exposure to wealth and success will breed a certain sense of entitlement. This, in turn, results in a lack of respect for others which is far worse than having an attitude.

Attitude is everything in business. We all know that attitudes come in hundreds of types. A person may change theirs many times daily. However, that's not really what I am describing here. What I am describing is like always having a certain chip on your shoulder, no matter what situation you are in … having swagger or an inner confidence that tells people "I'm here to stay so what are you going to do about it?" People will have sensed and know exactly where you are going and where you came from at all times. Swagger is having a self-presence at all times. There is never a day with nothing to do. At the least, there is always something to improve upon in your life. That's the "attitude" I am talking about. Trust me, there were many times where I was in a meeting where I wasn't totally correct in what I was saying, but my attitude was so convincing that it really didn't matter at the time. Like I have repeatedly written in other chapters, "We are here to make money, not to make friends. Our friends are at home." That, my friend, is ATTITUDE!

I probably have hundreds of stories in my life in where I interjected a little bit of "Brooklyn" when conducting business. However, I have a really good story that I think you will find entertaining and also show you the effectiveness of "The Brooklyn Show." This story is 100% true.

"The Five-Gallon Rule"

I was a couple of years into owning my own business, when I got a call from a very wealthy client of mine named Mr. C. This client asked me to come to his office to pick up a payment for some work we had completed at one of his properties. Mr. C was an older man with lots of money, and a person who was used to getting whatever he wanted, whenever he wanted it. In others words, he was the King of his Castle and that's how he liked it. If he liked you, then you could do no wrong. But if he didn't like you, then you could do no right.

When I showed up to his office at around 1:00 p.m., it happened to be Mr. C's birthday that day. Upon entering this beautiful wood-paneled office, I was immediately invited by him to join them at the conference room table and sit next to the boss for a piece of birthday cake. In the room, there were about 10 people, all employees of this company, and myself smack dab in the middle of it.

Upon saying my hellos to everyone and chatting in the background like a typical party gathering, I was asked by Mr. C the routine question that all business owners get from one another, "How's business?" I told him things were great, and that I was very happy how my company had grown. He responded with, "I am proud of you kid. Make sure you get paid from everyone you work for. Especially that guy over there with the big house on the corner! Not everyone is like me and pays their bills right away." Note that Mr. C was also the mayor of a wealthy nearby town, and had seen my trucks working on a large new home being constructed by another wealthy man he was not too fond of. So, without skipping a beat, I responded, "I'm not worried. I live by the five-gallon rule." So, looking very confused in his expensive suit, he said exactly what I was waiting to hear, "What the hell is the five-gallon rule?" That's when all the chatter in the room stopped and all of the employees were focused on my answer to a boss whom readily heard what people wanted him to hear. With a straight face, work clothes, baseball cap and boots, I leaned back on his office chair and said, "The way I see it in my world Mr. C, if you beat me for $5,000, then shame on me. But life goes on. If you beat me for $50,000, then I may hire an attorney, take you to court and try to get it. But still … life goes on. If you beat me for $500,000 or an amount where my life cannot go on as it has, then I will burn down your home with five gallons of gas purchased at the nearest gas station." When the last word came out of my mouth, there was sheer silence and shock from everyone in the room. The only thing you heard was the whizzing of the air conditioning duct.

At that moment, I had just injected them with a little bit of "Brooklyn" in business. Half of the people thought I was joking and the other half thought I was nuts. Either way, it didn't matter to me because they were on tilt going forward in our business relationship. To make sure that Mr. C hadn't taken it in the wrong way, I said to him, "Look, all I am saying is that a man who has much should never get another man to a point where he has nothing to lose. A man with nothing to lose is a very dangerous man for that exact reason. He no longer cares, and therefore, if you are a result of his losses, then he will make sure you feel what he is feeling." Mr. C looked at me and said, "I understand your point," so I smiled at him and said, "What are you worried about? You're my best customer!" That kind of relieved the situation and brought everyone back to party chatter.

Was I really going to burn down someone's home? No. But I can truly say this with conviction that if a person with huge resources used those resources to hurt me to a point where I was nothing, then I would have nothing to lose. My intent in telling the "Five-Gallon Rule" story to Mr. C was this. Here is a professional man with lots of money, surrounded by "yes people" because he is paying them. After years of exposure to this, I am absolutely sure Mr. C operated in a surreal state of mind, a state where life in general was one big Disney World for him with a nice house, nice car, political power and not one monetary problem. The story was a reminder to him that nobody, and I mean nobody, is above it all ... no matter how much money you have. So if his plan was not my plan, then he better watch out for the right hook!

CHAPTER 11

Know What You Have

"Money is the prize, not the source of your ambition. So love what you do and it is never a job."

I guess just by purchasing this book, I assume that you may have bigger aspirations for yourself then where you are now. It should never be a negative to want to better yourself; not at work and especially not in life. However, many often get delusions of grandeur and feel like that even though things are going pretty smooth at their current job, they are missing out on something much better somewhere else. Everyone, and I mean everyone, who has worked for someone in their life, has, at one point or another, come to an emotional crossroad of deciding on either staying where they are or leaving their job for something better.

There are instances where money is not even the primary reason for wanting change. Sometimes, quality of life issues propagate themselves at certain points in your life and force you to decide on career or life. The other day, I was speaking to my childhood friend, Dominick, on the phone who had just landed in Boston on a business trip. Dominick works for a pharmaceutical firm in their finance department directly under the supervision of their CFO. Dominick is one of the neighborhood guys who made it out of the blue collar world he grew up knowing and became a successful business executive in his own right. With a bachelor's degree in accounting, CPA and years under his belt as an accountant with a big six accounting firm, Dominick has spent the last 10 years of his career in the suit and tie world of pharmaceuticals. Even though I am not in his shoes, I can imagine that his daily grind may not be that of his dads and his brothers who run a local landscaping business in the neighborhood. In the eyes of many, Dominick is already living the American dream: "Suit and tie with a nice comfortable paycheck." He lives a business life that includes a nice paycheck, big meetings, air-conditioned conference rooms, corporate cards, corporate travel and dining out. So what surprised me when we were on the phone is how lost or indecisive Dominick was feeling about a career which I or anyone else for that matter were jealous of. He explained to me that the corporate world was nice, but since getting engaged to his longtime girlfriend, he has had different feelings of what would define his career. Dominick's dilemma is a struggle between family and quality of life versus a career and big paycheck. This is not just Dominick's problem, but it's one of the most common modern day dilemmas that each working person encountered or will encounter in their life. Women encounter similar issues when wanting to start a family and raise children in lieu of continuing their career. Whether you are male or female, these choices are tough and require time and patience.

The purpose of this chapter is to make sure you clearly "know what you have" at your current job before you go off and make some decision that you might regret later on. I want you to look at all the angles of your current job and the risks and rewards of taking a leap into something else. Sometimes, one's own ambition can blind them from seeing the obvious poor choices they are making. Hopefully after reading this chapter, you can better formulate your current position and then decide on what path to take in your career.

Have you ever been at a point in your career where you have entertained switching jobs or considered something even more dramatic such as switching careers? If you have been in the corporate workforce long enough, I am almost sure that you have muttered or heard these lines before, "They offered me:

- ► More money ...
- ► A higher title ...
- ► Better hours ...
- ► Company perks ... etc., etc.

All of these reasons seem to be valid enough to entertain the idea of switching jobs. However, before rushing out the door with your briefcase in hand, it is important to know exactly what you have now in your employment, and I don't mean in salary alone.

There is a difference between a career and a job. A "job" is a task for someone; while a "career" is a way of life for someone.

Sometimes in a long career, you can hold various jobs within it and still be successful. For example, the manager of a local supermarket could have started their career 20 years earlier stocking shelves, moving up to cashier, then department manager and finally, store manager. Each one of those roles I just described was a job in a long, successful career. The individual may not have loved all the jobs they had during those years, but they loved what they did then and still loves what they do now.

The very first thing about "knowing what you have" is to look at your career a whole first. I know I have mentioned this numerous times in this book before about "loving what you do." Take just a moment to reflect on your current employment and scrape away all the little annoying things that may be making you look elsewhere. Imagine that all the negative issues were resolved and things were perfect and ideal. Would you absolutely love what you are doing? Or is it that no matter what adjustments are made at work by your company or you and your family at home, you will never be truly happy? If the actual job does not make you happy with all scenarios being perfect, then your current career is not for you. It is my opinion that you immediately look into careers that may make you happy doing them, even if you were not getting paid. The intent is not for you to throw caution to the wind and join the circus leaving real world responsibilities behind. Remember that your success is still based on your need to get up and go to work and produce for some company somewhere, following all of the rules written in previous chapters in this book. It doesn't mean that because you always wanted to be a rock star, that you should drop your career to become one. We are not talking about chasing dreams, but rather, establishing a career as a way of life. It's a huge difference between the two (Chapter IV: Create Goals, explained this in detail). It is obvious we all have real world obligations like family, children, mortgages, taxes, bills, bills and more bills. Therefore, if you are legitimately putting in the time and effort at your current job and still feel like something is missing, then the career choice you have made is not the correct one. If you are already putting the time in and are working hard, getting there on time, producing, etc., then you are already completing the hardest parts of being successful on a daily basis. The only thing left to do is replace the career itself, so that getting up in the morning to go to work feels natural to you rather than a mundane task. Knowing what you have is very important to the longevity and health of your career.

Your career deserves the same level of respect as your wife or husband. How many times do we say in relationships, "You don't know what you have until it is gone." Well, your career is that high school sweetheart that you dumped and ends up marrying your friend, and you are sitting at home wishing you had her back. This is why it is important to never believe that you are greater than the career itself and that you deserve or can find better without any substantiation of such thoughts. Let us begin the "knowing process" by breaking it up into three major categories.

1. What to change

Is it the job or is it the career? Follow your heart, it will not lie to you. You know the answer already, but let's make that decision together right now. If you paid attention at the start of this chapter and in previous chapters, then you already have a pretty good grasp of where you are, what you are worth, and where you want to be in the future. If the future does not paint a picture with your current career in it, for whatever the reason, then it is time to change and get you on the path of success. The best way to describe it is that your career is the field or specific industry that you will dedicate your life to, and the jobs are the different levels within that field. I have heard this many times before from others, "I love what I do, but I hate what I'm doing." At first, it sounds confusing, but the more you think about it, it is saying that the person loves their career but hates their current job.

2. The decision process

What is it that you want? What are the things you are yearning for that will validate you in making a change at your job and career. Pinpointing exactly what you need changed in your current career is the key to understanding if you should make that change in the first place. For example, if you feel like you are being underpaid for what you are doing, then increased pay is what will validate your decision. These criteria can be almost anything you feel that you are missing at the current job or at home, and that if it were being fulfilled, you would not even think of switching that job. Take a minute to write down the first things that come to your mind immediately "as to why you are looking somewhere else." You can have hundreds of wants that you can write down, but once you have your first list completed. Go through each item on the list and split them into two major categories "Work-Related" and "Home-Related." Here are some typical examples:

Work-Related	Home-Related
More money	Shorter commute
Health benefits	Raise children
Position/title change	Reduce spousal stresses
Company car/other perks	More family time
Work environment	More vacations
Weekends off	Health and fitness
No more travel	Cost of living

The next step is to take the many wants you have written into your two categories and begin comparing each of them to one another, and then to your current status of employment. Begin the process by reading each of your wants and rate them on a level of one to five, with five being the most important to you in making your decision. Do this for both sides of your list.

Work-Related	SCORE	Home-Related	SCORE
More money	5	Shorter commute	2
Benefits	3	Raise children	5
Position/title change	2	Reduced spousal stresses	3
Company car/other perks	1	More family time	4
Work environment	3	More vacations	2
Weekends off	4	Health and fitness	3
No more travel	2	Cost of living	1

Now, rewrite your list by putting the most important wants' highest number first. With this being completed, you can clearly compare and see what items are most important to you at work and the effect it may have on your personal life at home.

Work-Related	SCORE	Home-Related	SCORE
More money	5	Raise children	5
Weekends off	4	More family time	4
Work environment	3	Health and fitness	3
Benefits	3	Reduced spousal stresses	3
No more travel	2	More vacations	2
Position/ title change	2	Shorter commute	2
Company car/other perks	1	Cost of living	1

With the list rewritten in the order of importance, begin the process of describing each one and the current situation that you are in. I have written in some examples below:

Work-Related	Description	Home-Related	Description
More money	Based on my reading of the chapter "Know your Worth," I believe that I deserve a raise in the 10% range.	**Raise children/more family time**	I have two young children who are participating in after-school curriculum and I would like to be there for those tee-ball games.
Weekends off	I have no weekends off.	**More family time**	We don't spend enough time as a family because of our work schedules.
Work environment	I feel that the environment I am in at work is too hostile and cutthroat.	**Health and fitness**	I gained a lot of weight in the past few years, and my sugar intake and blood pressure are up.
Benefits	Even though I get health insurance, there is no profit sharing, or 401k plan to participate in.	**Reduce spousal stresses**	Because of my work schedule, my wife is stuck doing most cooking, cleaning and parenting.

Work-Related	Description	Home-Related	Description
No more travel	I fly constantly from city to city, which keeps me away from the family.	**Shorter commute**	My current commute is three hours a day, which is both killing my personal time, and my wallet with the cost of gas.
Position/title change	My responsibilities mirror those of management but I have yet to be given such a corporate title.	**More vacations**	We haven't taken a vacation since our honeymoon.
Company car/other perks	I currently have to use my personal car for my commute, and the car is old. I would like to continue my education but it's very costly.	**Cost of living**	Our current cost of living is high because of where we live.

Validation

With your list compiled and complete, you now have a clear vision as to what is important to you and what impact a career change or change in employment will have on each one of the criteria (wants) you have indicated. One thing that truly becomes apparent to you is that all of your wants will almost never be satisfied, and they sometimes work against one another. The clearest example and most common one is when a person gets a pay raise, they usually sacrifice the things that may be the most important to them, like spending more time at home. An employer will pay more, but expects more, and it almost never happens that you get paid more to spend less time at work. It is usually a tradeoff between the two. That is why I made you create this list on paper, so it is visual and in your face. Each and every "want" you have written on the work-related side directly correlates to the "want" on the home-related side. Any change by you on either side of the chart will have a negative or positive effect on the other side.

Now, the key is to truly validate your decision in making a change by going through every possible scenario and effect that may occur when you manipulate one of the "wants" on either side for your benefit. For example, if you really don't work weekends any more, then you will have a positive effect on being more with your family, but it will mean a negative effect with a reduction in pay, and it may result in longer period for promotion. If you don't mind the negative effect as much as the positive, then your decision is crystal clear. But you need to go through dozens of scenarios and mental algorithms to come to a final conclusion if that change is truly warranted. Once the process of making that change begins, it is very difficult to ever turn back that decision because, as you can see, it affects both work and family which is your life.

If you might not be looking for that career change, but rather just validate a change of job instead, a good tool is to take these "wants" with you when you go interview with another company for the same job. I am not suggesting to pull out this list and use it to negotiate your wants, but rather, bring it with you mentally and reflect on what questions you need to ask during that interview process to make the right decision in staying or going. All of the data you gather during the interview can be taken back with you and you can go through the whole exercise of analyzing the true pros and cons of each. That's why I would never recommend accepting a job on the spot, before actually completing this exercise.

It is funny to see friends of mine who quit their jobs for more money, but never realized that they are working more, traveling more, spending less time with their family, or even worse, having to relocate away from their family. Their income may have risen, but their quality of life may have diminished considerably. Like I said in the introduction of this book, your goal is to find "a better Ying and Yang." That is to maintain a delicate balance between career (The Ying), quality of life (The Yang), and maximizing the salary (the better) between the two.

How to Change?

You did the exercise and you looked at all of the scenarios and have concluded that, in your heart and on paper, it is time to make that change. The next step is finding out exactly how to execute that change.

If you decided on a career change, then revisit Chapter IV on "Creating Goals" and strengthen your perspective on what these goals are and how to achieve them. The last thing I want you to do is go for the career change and start off in a job that has no real impact on achieving your goals. Like I explained in Chapter IV, the different goals you create need to tie into one another like rungs on ladder, with the top of your ladder being the achievement of your ultimate goal in that career. The jobs you take are the steps and energy you put in to climb up that ladder. The rate in which you ascend that ladder is up to you and the effort you put into it. It's that easy. I read a chapter in the book *The Secrets to Success* by motivational speaker Eric Thomas where he tells of how he finally had wound up in a good place in life, with a good job and family, and decided to give it all up, relocate his family and go back to school to pursue the career he had in his heart. To Eric Thomas, money was secondary to his goal. He followed his heart, put in the work and dedication required, and achieved his dreams. Today, he is doing exactly what he loves to do, and today, you need to decide what you love to do!

If you really love your career, but hate the job you are currently at, then the decisions you make may not be as drastic as you think as in the situation of a career change. First, based on the list of wants you made, do you think your current employer could make some changes within their company so that you can stay there and continue on with your goals? More often than not, if you go into your employer and you clearly "know your worth" ahead of time and state your case based on all of the exercises described above, I am sure that your boss will be more than accommodating. Successful companies and bosses are not in the business of pushing out great employees such as you. Quite the opposite is true. They want to retain their best employees without giving away the farm. If you "know your worth" (re-read Chapter VII), what you might be asking may surely be within the realm of possibility. Never ask above that imaginary ceiling what you are worth because you will never get it.

I am a big believer in staying with the company you are with for as long as possible and always working out the differences. Companies like to accommodate great employees and sometimes they may not budge on your pay, but may make improvements on some of your quality of life issues. If you look at the big picture and don't quantify everything with the paycheck alone, you might find yourself in a better position by staying with your current employer rather than going to work for someone else. If you are fixated on making the most money as fast as possible, then you should be aware of those pitfalls.

Jumping around from company to company may provide some immediate increases in pay, but can backfire on you in the long run. When the hiring market is strong, employers will run up the salaries to recruit and retain their employees. If you want to make more money faster, then the quickest way to do so is to jump to another company. However, when the economy cools, you are usually the first one back on the street. Companies would rather keep their most senior employees who have a long history with their company than a hired gun who came on board asking for lots of money. Jumping around at work is like the girl in the neighborhood that gets around … you're good for the moment, but over time, your reputation gets out, and in the long run, nobody wants you. Its absolute fact that hiring managers, when reviewing resumes, focus specifically on the amount of time you have spent with your previous employers. The reasons for leaving are less important than the actual time served. How can someone looking to hire a good employee trust the fact that this prospect has held three different jobs within the past three years? In my opinion, employment tenures of five years or less paint a negative picture, regardless of the reason for leaving. Multiple jumps within a year or two should be a dead giveaway of a bad seed and employers need to steer clear of such an employee.

However, if you have exhausted all of your internal options with your company, and yet you still feel unfulfilled based on the exercises you completed, then it is time to move forward and make that change. If you have fulfilled your obligation to your current employer and they have failed to make some attempt at accommodating you, then it is time to move on and make that change. Get on the phone, get out and interview and find the right fit to achieving your goals. Make sure that you weigh all of your options. Don't look for immediate satisfaction, but rather, long-term success as you will find yourself in a much happier place where you can continue to do what you love.

CHAPTER **12**

Second Fiddle Is Unacceptable

"In business, the person holding the dollar always makes the decisions. So learn to identify who that individual is or become that individual."

When you Google the idiom "To play second fiddle," it is described as follows: "Someone who is in a stronger position or is more important than you." This, in any System, should never be acceptable to you. Second place is the first loser, and you should never accept being number two in any position you hold in any company, at any level within its System. This feeling of always striving to be number one and never accept playing second fiddle should run deep in your veins and power you to strive and succeed.

I believe that successful people, both consciously and subconsciously, strive to be number one and thrive at being the ones calling the shots. The passion to be the best is the fuel that keeps the motor running, and it is what truly drives successful people. It's not money alone. Money, and lots of it, is the byproduct of being the best. When you are the best at what you do, there is no better option out there for your employer, therefore, making you the most valuable asset in that position. The result is an ascent up the corporate ladder, an increase in salary and/or both. The increase in position will make you a subordinate again, but at a higher level within the System. It is up to you to repeat the process and strive to be number one within that tier again without becoming complacent. By repeating the process repeatedly, the end game will result in three possible outcomes: (1) A partnership within your company; (2) Replacing the current CEO; or (3) Leaving and starting your own company.

Most corporate Systems are set up to create an environment of teamwork, and have multiple management layers within them which slow down one's true ability to shine. Teamwork is essential to any System. However, it us up to you as the individual to prove yourself as a leader within that team. It's just like when a sports team puts a "C" for captain on one of its players. It means that this player, who is part of the team, has been assigned to call the shots because he or she is their leader. They follow the captain who speaks for the rest of the team, and they are mutually respected for this by the coach of the team. It's not always a monetary reason for wanting to be a leader, but at least 90% of the time, the best player on a team is also the team captain, and that individual also happens to be one making the most money. There are exceptions to these rules, but like in sports, underperforming captains are usually replaced or traded for ones who do perform.

If you take a look at the company you are currently working for, you can see the different management layers within your company until reaching the CEO position. At each layer of management, you are playing second fiddle to someone else above you on the corporate ladder. The key is to not accept being stuck at any particular level, but instead, doing what is necessary to continue your rise upwards. Remember, like I have stated numerous times in this book before, complacency kills, and if those above you are accepting of playing second fiddle to someone else, it will be a matter of time before they are working for you.

Corporate Systems thrive when great employees are content at being told what to do. However, what they must also realize is the few rouge employees with fire in their veins who are not looking to settle down, need to be harnessed or find themselves in future competition with these individuals.

Many of today's successful CEOs were once employees of a competitor, and when their System no longer sustained that individual, they left to create a better System of their own somewhere else. It happens all of the time.

I guess by now, since we are in the 12th Chapter of this book, complacency is no longer in your vocabulary either. Are you sure? Take a break from reading for a bit and reflect on whether you really have that passion I have described or are you really content at marching to the beat of someone else's drum.

I am going to tell you a few stories of my past experiences. If any of these experiences are exactly what you feel in similar situations, then you share the same internal fire to never be number two, but always strive to be number one at any level.

Let's put it this way, it took me a long time to figure out why I am never content, and always striving to be the best at whatever I set my mind to. However, after having children of my own and reflecting on my early years, I have begun to see what made me the way I am.

At first glance, if you speak to my friends, they say it's the money that makes him tick. "He loves money," they are likely to say. Well, it is true … I do love money. However, when you speak to those who share similar passions as mine, it's not the money itself that drives them, but rather, the process of making it. Money may be the prize, but it is not the source of my ambition. It is the thrill of the deal that releases the endorphins that drive me, not the money itself. The money validates the hard work and passion you put into what you are doing. The more money you make, the more it validates you, which perpetuates the cycle for you wanting more. Money allows you to spend it in any way you want in order to reaffirm your passion and galvanize your existence as a human being. For example, in my life, I have met successful people who are tough as nails and are very hard to deal with when it came to their money. One person that comes to mind is my brother in-law, Phil, who is a very successful builder and attorney.

Business is business

Phil, like many successful people before him, has the ability to keep business as business no matter who the person he is dealing with. I remember not too long ago, he had partnered up with a friend to build a multi-unit apartment building in Queens and had approached me to give him a price on the plumbing work for that building. I personally spent a few days analyzing his drawings and preparing a bid to make 100% sure I was doing the best work for the best possible price for both him and I to be happy.

Upon meeting with him and his partner, I was first awarded the job and then the next day, the job was taken away and awarded to someone else because the numbers were better. It didn't matter to Phil that I was his brother-in-law, nor did it matter that I was definitely going to do a better job. It didn't matter that he was going to make a large amount of money on the project anyway (which paled in comparison to what my difference was in price). The fact was that it was all about the numbers and the numbers only. Yes! It hurt not getting that job, because its impact to my company was more than what it was on his wallet. However, in the long run, I respected him for that decision. By him saving whatever money he thinks he saved (or really did save), Phil had to decide just how to spend it. That's where the dichotomy of Phil's mindset, and others like him, comes into play. You see, where he plays second fiddle to no one when conducting a business deal, he finds no problem allowing those he cares about in reaping in his rewards. The same ruthless businessman I just spoke about can turn around a give you the shirt off his back if you were in a jam and needed it. I never got his project, but he never spared any expense when it came to me or my family. To this day, he treats my kids as if they were his own, and I respect him for that. In the long run, when looking back at the situation, I thank him every day for teaching me a lesson and not making things personal.

I too share my brother-in-law's passion for business. Therefore, it should be no surprise to you that I went on to have a banner year, despite never getting his project. If business is business, then it was up to me to go get it, because it was apparent that no one was going to give it to me.

When you are in the corporate System, your only loyalty is to the System itself and nothing else. Like I have written in previous chapters, "There are no friends at work. "As long as you let the System in place guide your actions and not make it personal, then your success is imminent. I am sure that you have heard the term before, "He means business." Well, you should always mean business when you are at work. That's what successful people do. They implement the Systems in place for them to succeed and rarely break the rules, unless there is something bigger within the System. In other words, if they stray from company protocol, they don't look at it as a favor for someone, it is considered an investment in their eyes. They are always looking for a return on something … it's just in their blood as it should be in yours. "In business, favors are forgotten, but scores are always kept." Always remember that motto!

It doesn't hurt to ask

We were in Aruba on vacation a few years ago when Phil received a call from a contractor who had finished his job and was looking to pick up the balance of his contracted amount. Phil, without skipping a beat, quickly answered him as follows, "What's the balance I owe you? Thirty-three hundred? You think we can do a little better, like three thousand? I will have my secretary cut you a check today and you can go pick it up. Yes? Okay, great! Go get the check! Thank you, and I will see you when I get back."

When Phil hung up the phone, I turned to him and asked, "Didn't you have an agreed price with him before he started the job?" He responded with, "Yes, of course." I asked why he took off that money if he already knew what was owed. Phil turned to me with a smile and replied, "Because I would hate myself later if I didn't ask." To Phil, it wasn't about the amount of money, but rather, the thrill of negotiating the best possible outcome at the very last minute. Even on vacation, he couldn't control his passion to negotiate. Rainmakers (aka, successful people like Phil) follow one major rule in the negotiating process: "In business, the person holding the dollar always makes the decisions. So learn to identify who that individual is or become that individual."

Phil knew he was the guy holding the money, and the ability for him to release it immediately made it appetizing for the contractor to reduce his price and so he did. Rainmakers know money today is worth more than money tomorrow. Just like when the lottery gives you your winnings upfront, they take a much larger cut. Looking at Phil's transaction in saving $300 doesn't seem like a big deal, but when you look at the big picture, the numbers become staggering. Let's round it off to a 10% saving by his negotiating. Then, take the 10% off his total monies spent among all his construction projects in year. Using round numbers, if he does $10 million annually in construction, he actually negotiates himself $1 million for "just asking!"

I, like Phil, try to negotiate the best possible deal for myself. The difference between me and him is that I prefer to do the negotiating before the start of a contract and not at the end. Phil does it on both ends of deal, because he just has to. It's in his blood to make sure that he is getting deal number one, not deal number two. The funny part was that he told me "If he wouldn't have budged, I still would have gave him the money."

If you like to negotiate, then you don't like to play second fiddle. If you want to be a successful person, then you need to learn to ask for things. Is that crazy? You need to ask for things? That's correct. Asking for things is its own art form, and it's up to you to learn how to do it correctly based on each situation. There is one thing I am sure about, however, that everyone must do when asking for something … always to do it in person. Mano-a-mano

.... Eye-to-eye. No texting, no e-mailing and not via voicemail. Based on the importance of the negotiation, it is always better to negotiate in person because one can play off another and get the instant feedback to come to an early resolution. When navigating through the corporate System, you encounter daily situations where you may need to ask for something of someone else. That is purposely set up that way because the System cannot possibly have a rule in place for every situation. In fact, most systems are set up to allow for negotiations, and it's the rainmakers who remember to ask for what they want. They don't assume the other person knows. So they ask instead. By asking of someone, you put that person in your mindset. Once that person is thinking at your level, then it's much easier to negotiate the outcome in your favor.

Personal Validation

My earliest memories of me not accepting playing second fiddle began during my childhood. I clearly remember sitting around the kitchen table waiting for my dad to come home from work and present him with my 98% test score. As soon as I gave him that paper, the outcome was not your typical answer. Instead of him telling me how proud he was of my score, he would ask me who in the class had a higher score. I would always tell him that my buddy Jose (who was extremely bright, and a doctor today) had scored a perfect 100%. So his next question was why I hadn't scored a perfect grade like Jose did. I waited for many years for my dad to validate me and it never came. The result of him always wanting more from me indirectly made me want to give it to him. While many might have used my dad's unconventional parenting style as an excuse to give up and fail, I used it as the fuel to prove to him that I was going to be my own success on my own terms.

My dad, like I have mentioned throughout this book, was an Italian immigrant living in a country that gave him no free passes, but offered lots of opportunity for his family based on his hard work. I remember him telling me that, in life, if you don't suffer, then there is no joy. What he meant was, you had to work hard to reach your ultimate goal. It is hard work that validates you in expressing that joy of achievement. If things come too easy, than you are not working hard enough or are selling yourself short with artificial and easily-attainable goals. In other words, if he had told me that a grade of 98% was acceptable, then what would I be looking for the next time I took the test? Would I really want to put the time in to get a score of 100%? And if I scored a 96%, would it be just as acceptable as scoring a 98% since we weren't striving for the perfect score anyway? As I got older, I started realizing that I was living my life, but also living my dad's life as he would have wanted to live it if he had the same opportunities as I had available. All I really wanted from him was to tell me he was proud of me, but since I was not getting the validation from him directly, I set out to prove it on my own terms.

Being validated, meaning that your own existence has some value in at least one other person's eyes, may serve as the fuel that flames your internal fire as it did to me. How many stories have you read of successful people who, when interviewed, say that they did what they did for their mother, their father, their coach, their teacher, or any other individual in their lives who validates their accomplishments. There are exceptions where individuals often become number one on their own terms without any outside validation, but instead, use their own success to assist others. This process of self-validation achieves the same result for successful people, but instead, they do it by using their available resources to positively impact the lives of others.

Very wealthy people begin to realize that money alone will not fuel their passion for too long. Once you have money, that can pretty much buy anything your heart desires, then what exactly will your heart have left to desire? This is the reason that people like Bill Gates and Warren Buffet give away most of their money to help others. It validates their existence on this planet, and continues to fuel their fire to continue to be successful. Their passion doesn't change, but their version of success does. Bill Gates might have felt, 40 years ago, that a being the richest person on the planet was his passion and nobody was going to stop him. After being that person for the last 20 years, I guess being the richest person in the world is not important if you cannot help cure Malaria.

Validation is different for every person operating within each corporate System. In general, validation is usually money- or title-related, but over time as your rise within a System, it becomes more of a personal validation. No matter what, always find exactly what motivates you to achieve greater things and never settle. If you can find what validates your existence, than you can fuel the fire within to never accept being second fiddle.

I like nice things

The first-born, silver spoon baby, mamma's boy or any other term you can think of that can relate to a spoiled person can provide a certain benefit to wanting to be successful. I can speak from experience, because I was a first born son, a huge mamma's boy who was spoiled rotten by my Italian momma. My mom cooked and cleaned for me from the time I was born, up until the night before I got married at 27-years-old. I lived at home and she cleaned my clothes, folded my laundry, cooked whatever I asked for and cleaned my dishes. To this day, I still don't understand why I ever left home to get married!

I can remember my first year of engineering school at Manhattan College in the Bronx. I tried dorming at school. That lasted just one semester. Even though I was only 15 miles from home, I felt like I was living into another country. I was so homesick. I would go home every weekend and have my mom wash my clothes and bring in a new batch on Monday. Being the first child and also the first son, I was put on the "Beloved Pedestal" at birth by my grandma to be served upon by everyone at my beckon call. My mom nicknamed me "King Tut" at an early age because I was treated like a king by everyone in the family.

What does being spoiled have to do with not accepting to play second fiddle? It has everything to do with it. When you are spoiled, you are used to getting your own way most of the time, and when you don't get your way, it bothers you a lot. Well, that was me. I hated being number two in any situation, especially when I was number one in so many people's eyes. Yes, I was spoiled, but the difference was, and still remains, that I knew I was spoiled. I knew the difference, so I knew I was *privileged* to be spoiled and it was not *my right* to be spoiled. When you are aware of your surroundings and know how good you have it based on the sacrifices of those around you, then it should serve as the fire to strive for success and never settle for less. My parents gave me everything I ever wanted growing up, but they were transparent when giving it to me. I watched my old man with his plumbing business day in and day out, and my mother work another 40 hours at the bank, plus run the household and everything else in between. It was apparent that my good fortunes were a result of their hard work and not some trust fund bank account.

All people like nice things. It is inherent in all of us. I don't believe that it is a bad thing to grow up spoiled. I also don't feel that it is bad to want to be spoiled when you're an adult. Rich people are spoiled every day. It doesn't have to be their family that spoils them, instead, they use their money to pay people to do so. Successful people generally do not have to deal with life's mundane tasks because they have other people doing for them. This frees up their time in concentrating on becoming more successful. They have the money to pay people to do things they don't want to do themselves. As long as they properly compensate those doing the work, then what is wrong with wanting to be spoiled?

I feel that being spoiled and the ability to acquire nice things at an early age will ignite the fire within to want to achieve corporate success. The key is remembering that good things don't come from sky, but rather, come from hard work, dedication and a personal commitment. I believe that people sometimes get in trouble with the idea of wanting nice things when they lose respect of what it takes to acquire such things. If you acknowledge the hard work of your predecessors and make it your goal to work as just as hard to do better, then you will definitely never be anyone's second fiddle.

CHAPTER 13

Karma

"The toes you step on today may be connected to the ass you kiss tomorrow."

W hen I originally started writing this book, I wanted to write a chapter about ethics in business. However, the more I thought about ethics in business, the more I realized that one cannot write about ethics because who is to judge what is ethical or not in business. Therefore, a much more fitting name for this chapter would be "Karma." Karma, in its simplest form, is "you get what you give," and in the corporate world, and as it is in life, karma is something that you should never forget.

The successful businessman with lots of money has become a pariah in today's society. The advent of movements like Occupy Wall Street, and the media's depictions of such, has taken the prestige of success and made it a crime to want to succeed. Every time you turn on the television, successful businessmen are portrayed as greedy, self-absorbed, cutthroat individuals with no respect for others, much like the Gordon Gekko character in the movie "Wall Street." A steady barrage of negative media coverage has driven a giant wedge between "The Have" and "The Have Nots" in America, and has made it extremely difficult for those caught in between, aka the "middle class," to want to express their desire to become a success.

In a way, can you really blame the "Have Nots" to feel the way they do? In the past 10 years, we have seen gas prices quadruple, home values and wages plummet, healthcare costs skyrocket, and government fees (which are hidden taxes) eat up those much-needed everyday dollars. All of these aforementioned factors thus leave those who had a little with nearly nothing at all, while those who were in the middle with having much less. Some unfortunate members of the middle-class have fallen further than expected and have joined the "Have Nots." Today's America has the largest economic divide in this nation's history … an economic divide that grows by the minute. So when you turn on your local news and see them report on how the CEO of a certain company that lost billions was given a $20 million bonus, it's like pouring salt in their fresh economic wounds. Their resentment runs deep, and it's hard for anyone other than that CEO not to get angry. However, getting angry is not the issue, but how you act on that anger is.

One option is to march through the streets of Manhattan and squat in a park to prove a point. And just what is that point? To disrupt everyday working people from getting to and from work? What does that accomplish? Spectacles like Occupy Wall Street accomplish nothing, and it destroys their own credibility. If the Occupy Wall Street protesters had used the national media attention to establish their platform to cure America's problems, then it would all make sense. Instead, what we got was a melee of misguided individuals acting like spoiled brats looking for handouts from those who are successful and were deemed the elite "One Percent." These squatters are no better than that CEO, because they are both leeches to American society, but at different economic levels. For the most part, I firmly believe that out of a city of seven or eight million to have only a few thousand protesters shows that their percentage is not the 99%, but rather, far less than one percent. Just like the handful of CEOs who are making undeserved millions only reflect a tiny group of individuals in our nation's giant corporate system made up of many, both of these groups do not represent the norm, but rather, the exception, and neither of them deserve to be the representatives of American business.

America's corporate system is a capitalist system, with some government-imposed socialistic regulations. Capitalism, at its rawest form, has a direct parallel to survival of the fittest in the natural world. One must do whatever it takes to guarantee their own prosperity, and as a result, there will be casualties of success along the way. I would equate it to when you turn on the Discovery Channel and watch a herd of antelope running through the Serengeti being chased down by lions. The lions only catch and kill the slower and disillusioned ones, and unfortunately, the herd must continue to run along, leaving them behind to die. We, as humans, are animals ourselves, and are at the top of the natural world's food chain. Therefore, if we allow capitalism to run our society, it would mean letting the "Have Nots" starve and die in our own streets. It would mean only those with money would have access to food, water, hygiene, doctors and medication, thus leaving those with no money to fend for themselves.

Those who are born impaired or with maladies would be discarded immediately, leaving only the healthy to live and prosper in our society. Just reading this type of stuff is probably making you feel uncomfortable, because it gives me some discomfort as I write it. So, why does it makes us uncomfortable to think of this type of societal structure, even though as readers of this book we are fixated on our own ultimate success?

I believe the answer lies within our soul. It is our soul that keeps us from living in a truly pure capitalistic society. The human soul is distinctive to you, and it is what comprises you as person—not in the physical sense, but in the spiritual sense. It is your internal being that bases its decisions on the value of life as whole, rather than tangible things. All people, no matter their religion or race, have a soul. Each person, whether they be rich or poor, at one point or another in their lives, must come to terms with their own existence and why they were put here in this world in the first place. These moments usually occur at times where one experiences extreme non-materialistic happiness, such as the birth of their child, or during extreme sadness like the death of a loved one. When someone dies, no amount of money can bring them back, nor can they take their riches with them to spend in the afterlife. And when a child is born, that child only knows its love of its mother milk and warmth, not how much money sits in their parent's bank account. That is why armored cars do not follow hearses and you cannot buy baby formula at a bank.

In birth, as in death, we are all equal as humans. What happens in between the two is what we call life. For example, Bill Gates, at the time of his death, will be no better off than you or I when we die. Money and possessions have tangible value only here in physical world. Our life as we know it is the tangible, but our soul is there to remind us to pursue the intangibles.

Intangibles are things that we cannot count, measure or touch. There are the personal intangibles such as "love, kindness, compassion and empathy," and then there are the business intangibles such as "honesty, integrity, respect, pride and honor." Consequently, since your soul cannot be changed, then your life's intangibles are one in both your personal and business lives.

In theory, this makes lots of sense for those whose moral compass always seems to steer them to do the right thing. Unfortunately, the corporate world today is less about cleansing our soul and more about making a profit at all costs. One example that comes to mind is when a pharmaceutical company withholds or manipulates studies regarding the side effects of their product due to the potential financial windfall that can be made by selling it. Their numbers tell them that the billions that can be made far outweigh the potential payouts for lawsuits or deaths that may occur from putting their potentially harmful product on the market. What about the auto makers that knowingly send out vehicles to the market with known safety defects and worry about the lawsuits later? There are thousands of examples where corporate tangibles are put at the forefront of life's intangibles. What is even more unsettling is that it seems to me that in my short business life, I have seen corporate morality disintegrate at an even more rapid pace. Corporate structure, based on the credo of "Profit at all costs," has led to employees in the corporate System to "Go for theirs at all costs." Nobody wants to put in the hard work and dedication anymore. It's about getting to the top as fast as they can, no matter who or what may be negatively impacted along the way. Soul? What soul? They will worry about that later on after they make their millions!

All corporate Systems teach some form of ethics in business today. However, the thing that always gets me is who determines exactly what is ethical? That is the main reason why this chapter was not written on that premise alone. You might say to yourself when reading this, "Well what's so hard about writing being ethical? Just always do the right thing!" My question to you is then, "What is the right thing?" In life or death, it's pretty easy to figure out the right thing, but in business, what is ethical and what is unethical matters really by who is being affected by it. Still don't get it? Let me elaborate by giving some examples …

Let's make up a simple story and ask yourself what is ethical. Your friend is in the market of buying a used red car. They want a specific make and model and are willing to spend the going rate of $5,000 for that car. You, being in the auto business, happen to know another person who has that exact red car for sale for $2,500. What do you do? Do you just pass that information along and allow that person to sell directly to your friend? Do you purchase the car for $2,500 and sell it to your friend for $5,000? Or, do you purchase the car and sell it to your friend for $4,000 so that everyone wins?

What is ethical? Would it be ethical for you to make a profit because you needed the money? Or, would it be ethical for you to make a profit because the only reason you got the car so cheap was because you already had a long-standing business relationship with that person. Which means your friend would never get that opportunity to purchase it at that price. Or, do you make no money because that person is your friend and that's the right thing to do?

In my opinion, there is no correct answer. I will tell you how I see it, but you can disagree with the way I see it and still be correct. If it were me in this situation, I would have bought the car for $2,500 and sold it to my friend for $4,000. The only difference is that I would disclose all of the details of the transaction to my friend first by explaining why I got it so cheap, why he was being charged and why he was still ahead by $1,000. It would be a win-win situation for all parties. I feel that this is a business transaction first, and emotions should not play a part in keeping it business, even with friends. The reason for me getting that price on the car was because I was buying five other cars to sell at once. So I would not look at it as if that used car was a steal, but rather, it was the deal as whole that made it what it was. That meant I had to make the investment to reap its benefits. If I am the one making the investment and taking the risk on buying all of the cars, then my friend should understand that I need to make somewhat of a profit. Maybe not a profit as large as on the other cars, but I need to have that investment bringing in that return. If they are truly your friend, then I believe they should respect that decision. In reality, what was the only other option for your friend? Go and buy the car at full price or put up all the money to buy all the cars like I did?

My opinion on how to conduct business did not develop overnight. This whole concept of separating it as just business when dealing with people, especially those who you care about, sometimes may be a hard pill to swallow. Detaching your emotions from business decisions and balancing them with what your soul is telling you to do will be one of the keys to your corporate success. However, over time, those whom you truly love and care about and vice-versa will learn to respect your business, as well as the person.

I say it to many of my business colleagues today, "The term 'free' in business means it is, at minimum, done at cost." However, many see "cost" as the cost of that item only, or cost of the employee's hourly pay. In reality, true cost has to include overhead on top of that. So if you work for a mechanic and your dad comes in for an oil change, what should he really be charging your dad? The cost of the oil, the filter, and the $20 he paid you for the hour to do it? Or, should he include an upcharge for his rent, insurance, his vehicles, his parts, his office staff, his office supplies, his utilities and so on. Your boss might not want to make a profit on you, but he needs to cover his expenses or run the risk of going out of business. Each business works on a certain percentage of profit, and for each industry and business, this percentage varies. If you use an old rule of thumb of 30 percent profit on the oil change example, then the only discount you should be getting off the actual price is that 30 percent and nothing else.

Here is another example for you: Were the bankers during the mortgage boom acting ethically by giving mortgages to people who could not afford the properties they were buying? For those who went bankrupt, then the answer is "No." But what about those who were able to purchase a property under relaxed lending laws that were otherwise unattainable and are prospering today? I was one of them. I strongly believe that if I had tried to buy my business property today and not in 2007, I would have never received the financing I was approved for. I didn't go belly up, instead, I paid my bills, refinanced years later, and continue to prosper as a result of that initial loan. Were the bankers really to blame? Are you telling me all of these people never realized that they couldn't afford what they were doing? I find it hard to believe. Speak to a mortgage broker and they will tell you they were just "Fulfilling the American Dream of Homeownership." These mortgage brokers felt they were not being unethical at all. They did not break any rules, they simply sold the mortgage products that were on the marketplace at the time. I am, by no means, defending the housing crisis, but am just trying to prove a point as to what is ethical.

Bill Gates, the late Steve Jobs, Mark Zuckerberg and many others have made billions of dollars at the expense of others. There have been many lawsuits, movies made, and articles and books written on how these individuals and others like them got to where they are today. They made decisions along their path to success that may not have been ethical to those who suffered the consequences of those decisions. The larger these individuals and their companies grew, the more lives their business decisions directly impacted. Realistically, none of them can ever truly make an ethical decision because at any one time or another, one person may be benefitting by their actions and another may be losing dearly. Those on the losing end of things may not believe they are playing fair and might even call it unethical, but individuals such as Gates, Jobs and Zuckerberg just called it business.

In this chapter, we have identified the dichotomy of wanting personal success and being ethical in attaining it. However, like I stated in the first paragraph of this chapter, I believe that how you navigate through the corporate System as in life should be based on the understanding of "getting what you give" instead of figuring out what is right and what is wrong.

Karma, in my view, is life's great equalizer. As soon as you lose sight of the consequences of your actions, that's when your actions will come right back and kick you dead in the face. How simple is living and working by "getting what you give?" It's just that easy. This can be applied to anything you encounter on a daily basis at work. On the most general of levels, let's start by applying it to work ethic. The harder you perform at work, the more success you shall achieve. Your success will directly correlate to the time you put into achieving it. I remember reading a motivational quote on a wall that said: "Diligence is the mother of good luck–Benjamin Franklin." If I need to explain that quote, then you shouldn't be reading this book!

Karma, at any level, makes sense. Let's go back to the example of the used red car and selling it to your friend. I felt that it was good karma for me to be honest and upfront with the whole situation regarding the car and monies associated with the transaction. Nothing was left to the imagination by my friend or anyone else for that matter. Disclosing that information was the right thing to do for what I believed, and I felt that honesty is what I was giving in that transaction because I owed that to my friend and nothing more. Everything else regarding that situation was a business transaction and karma played no part in that. I gave my friend honesty, and all I expected in return from my friend was honesty as well. Maybe it was honesty at that minute on how he was feeling, or it was honesty later on in life where I may have been in need of it.

As for the mortgage brokers who sold all of those bad loans, I see that it is up to that mortgage broker to know for themself if they truly were out to make a homeowner's dream come true or if they were just lining their pockets. That's where the great equalizer of "KARMA" comes into the picture. Many of these brokers, bankers and financiers were bad people with no intention of helping anyone. Five-plus years after the economic crash and bottoming out of the housing market, karma has put many of these individuals out of business, in jail, or even worse, six-feet under. I don't have an answer as to what karma is, or who or what controls it, but I would never try to test its limits. Nature has a funny way of balancing things out on its own, and if you are operating in an area too far to one side, there will be a time where you will be forced to come to terms with the other side. Do you disagree? Are the Kennedys just prone to bad luck or is karma just balancing things out? Is Bernie Madoff paying his debt in jail, or did karma take his son's life as part of that debt? You get what you give. Remember this until the day you die. You might live your entire life taking instead of giving and can live through it all like a king. You might not be giving it back in your lifetime, but I am certain that karma will be taking it in your future children's and grandchildren's lives. So keep it simple, and remember, if you do good, you get good, and if you do bad, you will get bad.

In your life, as in business, do not try to overcomplicate and overanalyze situations that may arise. Instead, try to keep things simple and follow your gut instinct. It usually steers you in the right direction. And if you put your all in with no convictions in whatever you do, then you should never worry about the bad that can come, but rather, all of the good that karma shall bring. If you speak with honesty, give respect and maintain your integrity, then only good things await you. This does not guarantee monetary success, but it will give weight to your words and value to your name. No matter what economic success you have in business, it is your name that people will always remember you by, and karma will have an impact in those remembering your name.

CHAPTER 14

The Five Laws
To Conquer The System

Law #1: AMBITION
*"Have the **ambition** to go at the task at hand."*

Law #2: EFFORT
*"Put in the **effort** to complete the task at hand."*

Law #3: ABSORPTION
*"**Absorb** everything and anything in order to achieve that task at hand."*

Law #4: IMPLEMENTATION
*"Try to **implement** what you have learned to accomplish this task alone."*

Law #5: PRODUCTION
*"**Reproduce** the task efficiently and error-free, continuously."*

These five basic laws are the foundation to your success within any corporate System. This entire book has been simplified to these five laws. No matter where you currently are within the System, follow these five laws in precise order, and it will guarantee you continued growth and success within that System.

The term "task" within these laws are subjective to your interpretation. At its simplest form, the task can be something menial assigned to you by a superior within the System. Or, at its most complex form, the task can be a large project with many components with smaller tasks within it. It is not the situation you are presented with, but how you approach it. How you approach any situation will determine your success rate. In order for you to maximize your rate of success, it is vital to adhere to these rules.

If you didn't understand what the paragraphs above are trying to tell you, let me simplify it even further. Follow these five steps in any given situation at work and you will succeed. PERIOD! As you read these five basic laws, they may sound obvious to you already. You may already be practicing them on your own. This means you are a successful employee and even better things await you in the future. However, if you are currently not seeing the success rate at your job that you truly desire, then it would be in your best interest to take a subjective look at where you hit or miss with these five basic laws. It is very important to discern which one of these laws you are failing at and start improving at it immediately. Each one of these laws requires the same amount of attention, and an imbalance in any one of them will result in the failure of your task.

I thought about these five laws for years. They are written on a wall in my office in which I see and read everyday. To this day,

I cannot find a hole is this formula. If you think there is a better way than this, then I personally challenge you to show me otherwise. When you are done fooling yourself that you may know better, just remember to read the laws and descriptions below and live by them every second of every minute at work. You will not fail!

Law #1: AMBITION - *"Have the **ambition** to go at the task at hand."*

Everything starts with ambition. What is ambition? Based on a definition I found online, ambition is defined as: "An earnest desire for some type of achievement or distinction, as power or wealth, and the willingness to strive for its attainment." In a nutshell, your ambition is your will to work at something. That something can be anything at which you set your mind to. Each day, your job is comprised of many tasks. Some of these tasks are going to be repetitive and some will be new. It does not really matter what these tasks are. The key is to go at each one of them with the same willingness to complete them.

It reminds me (for those of you who have children) when you ask your child to clean their room. You immediately see that sour face and a rolling of the eyes as to not wanting to perform the task. Realizing they have no choice in the matter, they reluctantly drag their feet and proceed to clean their room. A boss, like a parent, can see right through you within seconds of asking you to do something. They already know if the outcome is going to be remotely close to what they expect. They see it your eyes whether or not that ambition is there or not. This lack of ambition lowers your bosses' expectations of success, thus leaving you to open to their scrutiny when the task is complete. Going through the motions because you need the paycheck and don't want to get fired is not a recipe for success, but definitely one for failure. To reluctantly complete a task to appease your boss and collect your money will result in the task getting completed in a manner which I like to call "half-assed." People who are doing half-assed work are also the first to bitch, moan and complain about the task in the first place. There is no place for whining in the work place ... whiners get fired!

Now let me ask you a question: What's the problem? Is it you or is it your boss? Don't answer because I am sure you don't think you are the problem ... but you are! What is wrong with the task? Is it too menial? Too easy? Too boring? Too anything? Yes, it probably is. So let me explain why it is like this. If it's your first time performing a particular task, then your superior is likely giving you a shot at something simple and/or something that someone else in the company doesn't want to do. They do this to test your mettle and see if you have the hutzpah ... aka "the balls," or the "ambition" to conquer this task. It is this reason why baseball recruits go to the minor leagues before they become stars in the major leagues. We all need to start somewhere and that "somewhere" is usually at the bottom. The bottom is where you prove to both your superiors and to yourself that you have the fire to do what it takes to achieve your final goal.

If you are given repeated menial tasks that you just cannot seem to get out of doing, then the only reason is that you are failing at one of the remaining four laws. Guaranteed! Fail at any one of these, and the entire System falls apart. If you are achieving your desired outcome based on the five laws, then it is your job to sit and meet with your superior and ask for a new challenge at hand. Sometimes, inept managers who are lacking in their own five laws, do not correctly identify those who are lacking as well and thus require a nudge from the bottom up. And like I have said many times before in this book, you will slowly take over their job if they remain complacent.

Remember, everything starts with "ambition." It is the internal fire that drives your engine. It's the mental, not the physical. The physical is part of Law #2, "Effort." Without ambition there is no fuel to power the engine that creates the effort. Therefore, begin the process to success by changing your mindset from negative to positive and let your goals lead the way.

Law #2: EFFORT - *"Put in the **effort** to complete the task at hand."*

How many of you have had or know a co-worker who talks up such a big game on what they are going to achieve and how they are going to achieve it? Yet these co-workers are the last ones to show up for work, the first ones to check the clock to go home, and are the biggest complainers of why they are being taken advantage of by the System. Some of these individuals are extremely intelligent and could really be as good as they think they are. However, with all of the ambition they display, they put in no effort towards acting on it. They have all the fuel in the tank, but the engine won't start because they are too damn lazy to turn the key. No matter if you are a boss or a horse at work, in order to be successful, one needs to put in the effort at achieving their tasks at hand. Everyone … no exceptions. Not even the boss.

Effort is the foundation to getting a positive outcome at achieving any task at hand. It's the "doing" in the equation of getting things done. To say it is one thing, but to actually do something is a much harder thing. Effort is the physical component to the ambition in Law #1. If you are missing either one, then your chances of a successfully completed task are zero to none. Get your ass out of that chair and do whatever it takes to accomplish what you have been given. If it requires reading, then read. If it requires research, then do research. If it requires physical labor, then provide the muscle needed. Whatever it is, there is no getting there late, there is no watching the clock and there is no complaining. Just work and get shit done!

Law #2 is the one that drives me the craziest, and the one that most people fail at miserably. They wonder why they cannot hold a job or wonder why they have low paying jobs, or can never move on from the position they are in. You know what is funny though? The writing is on the wall, and many refuse to see it, read it or accept it. Effort is everything. It is the cement in the step that you are building in the staircase to success. You cannot get to the top without taking the first step. Yet many do not want to believe it. How many success stories do you need to read or hear until it finally makes sense? If you want a direct correlation to your job, how about you ask your boss how they got started in the business and what they did to get to where they are today? Better yet, ask them about the mistakes they made rather than look at their successes. This way, you can better navigate your own success and direct your efforts, while avoiding the same pitfalls. It is a very rare situation that someone automatically starts at the top, and if they have, they usually don't maintain being at the top because they are missing that foundation (effort) to keep them up at the top.

Let me give you a basic example to better describe a different way at looking at why it makes absolutely no sense for someone not to put in the effort when accomplishing a task.

Let's say you have a job at a fast food establishment and your boss hands you a mop and asks you to go and mop the floors. You take the mop bucket, fill it up with water, and you use cold instead of hot. Why? Because the hot water handle is too hard to turn. You don't mix in the correct floor cleaner. Why? Because you cannot find it, so basic dish soap will do. You use an old mop head, and dirty mop bucket. Why? Because you don't want to touch the dirty stuff with your hands. You proceed over to the floor and begin to mop without sweeping first. Why? Because in your mind, this is a faster method and your friend just texted you and you need to go home and get ready to go out. Finally, you wet the entire floor into one big giant soup, and hope that it dries by the time your boss comes in the morning. Why? Because we are closing and its going to dry anyway so no need to dry the mop. Don't laugh at this scenario because it happens every day.

So, now you just rushed through a mopping task, but you still got it done in your mind, and yet you wonder why you are working for minimum wage? The next day, your boss walks in and knows exactly what you did wrong and asks an employee who believes in these five laws to mop the floor. Your co-worker doesn't meander. Instead, they put in the effort and mop that floor perfectly as they were taught during training. If we roll back the cameras and start a stopwatch simultaneously on both of you, the difference in time in achieving that task correctly or half-assed is inconsequential ... meaning there is very little difference in time when performing the task incorrectly instead of doing it right. Why? Because you still have to go through 95% of the steps anyway to do it wrong. The other five percent is what makes you a success or a total failure. That's it ... just five percent!

Effort makes up five percent of your time, but makes up 95% of your success.

I ask you right now to look down to your right hand and fold your thumb and your index finger (which is the finger closest to the thumb) and almost touch the tips together forming the letter "C" with like a quarter-inch air space between the two tips. That is my international symbol for the difference between being a "failure" and being a "success." That tiny space between those two fingers (hint: look at the books cover) is the amount of effort you need to put into every task to guarantee your path to success. Remember that symbol, and when your co-workers ask why you care so much about doing your job, show them that symbol. If they don't respect your effort, then give them the other international symbol and flip them the bird and let them know who is number one!

Law #3: ABSORPTION - *"Absorb everything and anything in order to achieve that task at hand."*

When you are given a task, and your ambition and effort are firing on all cylinders, what is the most important thing you need to remember? You were given this task for a reason, and all tasks always come with a dual purpose. The most obvious is to accomplish the task, but the second one is to actually learn that task. That's where absorption comes into play. You need to completely consume yourself into achieving that task at hand. It does not matter if you are going through the process with or without effort. If you do not absorb what you are doing to achieve that task, then the entire process was a waste of time. Employers want their employees to learn, and if they don't learn, then they cannot advance forward in the corporate System.

That is why when companies provide training, it is imperative that you absorb everything they show you. With all of the training videos, manuals and tutorials provided, it is up to you to immerse yourself in each and every step along the way to learn and perform that particular job at peak performance. Some smaller companies do not have training facilities. Instead, the boss is the instructor. That method, believe it or not, is not a negative, and is actually the best type of training any employee can receive. Working side-by-side with your boss leaves nothing to interpretation and allows you to absorb everything they tell you at every step in achieving an assigned task. Lastly, if your job does not have training and the people in place to train you have not provided enough for you to absorb, then it is up to you to either ask for more help or do it on your own. There are libraries of books, outside seminars, continuing education classes, conventions, trade shows, and unlimited data and videos on the Internet to help you absorb any task at hand.

The success of each one of these laws lies directly on the law before it. That is why the law of absorption sits right in the middle. The first two are the foundation to your success, but the third one is what allows you to maintain success every step along the way. As you absorb what you are doing, the job at hand becomes less of a job and more of a lifestyle. Learning to do things right the first time will actually take you more time to do it wrong just because you are not used to doing it incorrectly. Believe it or not, you learn to do things wrong just as much as you learn to do things right. That is why it is so important that your absorption begins immediately when being assigned a task, never allowing your mind and inexperience to fill in the blanks. It is this reason that the term "absorption" is being used in the third law. You are to absorb your surroundings to achieve your success, not improvise when you think there is nothing left for you to absorb. There is always something to learn at every level of corporate success. Always remember that a lack of absorption breeds ignorance, and ignorance guarantees failure.

Law #4: IMPLEMENTATION - *"Try to **implement** what you have learned to accomplish this task alone."*

When the training is complete and your boss is no longer around, this point becomes the make or break point for your accomplishing this task. You need to implement everything you absorbed and try to accomplish this task by yourself. Even though a good company has provided you with all of the tools you need to accomplish the task, in the end, it is always up to you to complete the task at hand. Implementation does not mean perfection the first time. Instead, it is where you have the ability to test what you absorbed, and judge to see where you may need improvement. I see the implementation stage of accomplishing a task as the beta test. This beta test allows you to make mistakes without being penalized for it. However, you must also realize that a beta test can only last so long until the boss pulls the plug on you and your task. The time frame for implementation is not endless, because companies are in the business of making money. The company always allots a certain amount of resources to its employee and its tasks. However, if implementing a task has used up too much of its resources, the employee will suffer the consequences, not the actual task. The company always wants its tasks completed and it will never change the task to accommodate an inept employee. The company would just replace an employee, and if that employee correctly implements the task given, then they will continue to rise up the corporate ladder. There is definitive time frame, so it is always in your best interest to learn and implement quickly because corporate America has very little patience.

In theory, if you did a really good job in the absorption process, then mistakes during implementation are minimal and your job is secure. During implementation, you continue to absorb new data as your experience grows and your confidence levels rise. When implementing, it is also a good opportunity for you to make your own recommendations within your company to improve a task and process even further. Like I stated earlier, everyone in the company has to follow laws, so this means that everyone has something new to absorb. If your recommendation proves to be an improvement to achieving that task more efficiently, then it is in your employer's best interest to accept it or be doomed by it later. There are many real world stories where an employee perfected what they had learned, but their boss was too stubborn to accept it. That employee eventually started their own company and put their old boss out of business. How about that for karma?

Law #5: PRODUCTION - *"**Reproduce** the task efficiently and error-free, continuously."*

If you followed the first four laws correctly, the fifth and final law of "Production" is a mere formality. It's like running the bases after hitting the game-winning walk-off home run. As an employee, the simplest translation of your job is to "produce." What you produce varies from job to job, task to task, and day to day. Your ultimate success is not predicated on how much you produce for the company alone. Instead, reproducing the assigned task must be done efficiently, free of mistakes and continuously replicated. At this stage, the beta testing is over, and it's go time. At this point, your boss no longer worries about you failing, but rather, waits to reap the benefits of your accomplishments. You and the task at hand are one. It is in your make up. The task has now become second nature to you.

"It is no longer a job it is a lifestyle."

The only thing that you should fear with the fifth law is the ability to handle the responsibility it has brought you. Many may follow all of the laws to the tee, and when they finally get to production, they crash and burn. It is not the work to reproduce that scares them away, but rather, the responsibility and accountability required to maintain it. Your company needs to make money and is relying on you to reproduce this task as long as you are their employee. They will not accept a regression in your performance because you are costing them money. However, every time you accomplish another fifth law, your value to the company rises. Your worth to them increases, and in turn, your pay increases, but so do your responsibilities. It is the weight of those responsibilities to maintain production that sometimes crushes the hopes of success. I have seen many good employees get exactly what they wanted, and once they arrived where they wanted to be, they realized it was too stressful and they quietly bowed out.

In conclusion, the five laws to "Conquer the System" are there for you to follow, but are to be used to your own limitations. When applying these laws continuously, your success is limited only to the amount of tasks you want to take on within the System. If you have what it takes and harness the fear of failure instead of running from it, you will conquer every aspect that the System has to offer.

Made in the USA
Charleston, SC
23 April 2014